CHANGE

WHAT HAPPENED

To you

How to Use Neuroscience to Get the Life You Want
by Changing Your Negative Childhood Memories

CHANGE
WHAT HAPPENED
To you

Odille and Steve Remmert

PowerstonePublishing.com

ISBN: 979-8-9852514-0-1 (print)
ISBN: 979-8-9852514-1-8 (ebook)
ISBN: 979-8-9852514-2-5 (audiobook)

Ordering Information:
Special discounts are available on quantity purchases by corporations, associations, and others. For details, contact Powerstone Publishing via their contact form at PowerstonePublishing.com.

Table of Contents

Introduction

Your childhood may be over…but your brain doesn't know that.

As far as the unconscious part of your brain is concerned, your childhood provides the "evidence" that "proves" who you are and how the world works. Change that evidence, and you change what you experience in your life, moving forward. Just like changing the coordinates in your GPS changes your destination.

This is not about changing how you feel about your past, and it's not about "reframing" what happened to you. This is about *changing* what happened to you.

The idea of changing memories may seem unfathomable, but that's only because you've probably not heard of it before. It is a relatively new area of research in neuroscience. The work we do in The Remmert Method is based on the research of scientists and researchers like Dr. Amy Milton, behavioral neuroscientist, fellow in neuroscience, and senior lecturer in the Department of Psychology at Cambridge University, who specifically studies memory reconsolidation ("memory editing"), and Dr. Julia Shaw, psychologist and research associate at University College, London. Dr. Shaw specializes in false memories. Memory reconsolidation[1] is already being used to treat post-traumatic stress disorder.

1   Jonathan Lee, Nader Karim, & Daniela Schiller. "An Update on Memory Reconsolidation Updating." Trends in Cognitive Sciences. 21(7), 2017: 531–45. doi:10.1016/j.tics.2017.04.006.

We have taken what we've learned about the effects of childhood memories on the adult, how brain chemistry is created, and the progress in the field of memory reconsolidation; experimented, by changing our own negative childhood memories; and have experienced complete transformational change. Since then, we have helped hundreds of clients to experience the same transformational change by changing their own negative childhood memories.

Our mission in sharing this information, and the aim of the step-by-step techniques and tools in this book, is to empower every individual to decide what they experience in their lives by choosing a *new* childhood that "proves" those results.

As is shown in Dr. Amy Milton's and Dr. Julia Shaw's work, the unconscious part of the brain can't tell the difference between reality and imagination, can't use logic or reason in the way the conscious mind can, and can't judge something to be unrealistic[2]. Considering this, it will accept any *new* "evidence" of who you are and how the world works, while you will still consciously know what originally happened. Just like changing the coordinates in your GPS—the GPS will accept the coordinates of the new destination while you, as the driver, can still remember your previous destinations.

It's the difference between implicit or nondeclarative (unconscious) memory and explicit or declarative (conscious) memory. We will show you how to change implicit negative childhood memories to the opposite, positive, and empowering, while shifting the original memory to declarative.

About the Authors

We are not doctors or scientists. In fact, before we found ourselves in the world of neuroscience and helping others to empower themselves (and long before we met), Odille was a professional actress and singer, and Steve ran his own business as a designer/ builder of custom-made furniture.

---

2   University of Colorado at Boulder. "Your Brain on Imagination: It's a lot like Reality, Study Shows." ScienceDaily. December 10, 2018. www.sciencedaily.com/releases/2018/12/181210144943.htm.

We had each struggled, throughout our lives, to "fix" ourselves. On our own personal journeys to find solutions for our problems, we would share what we learned and help others along the way. This led Steve to go back to university to do a psychotherapy degree, and Odille to become a life coach.

By the time we met, we were both using some of the techniques we now share in this book. The rest we developed together—through seeking solutions for ourselves and others, and by researching and putting together information we learned from various sources. We experimented by applying our findings to ourselves, to change our own lives, and then shared it with others. When we saw that our method worked equally well for others, we continued to develop it—to add to and improve on our techniques, to find solutions for our clients to help them overcome challenges and trauma, and to empower them to create the changes in their lives they were longing for.

Changing the World by Changing Childhood Memories

As humans, we have key instinctive priorities:

1. Our primary priority is survival[3]—if we don't survive, nothing else matters.
2. Our secondary priorities are connection, altruism, and helping others[4].

---

3   Dean Mobbs, Cindy C. Hagan, Tim Dalgleish, Brian Silston, & Charlotte Prévost. "The Ecology of Human Fear: Survival Optimization and the Nervous System." Frontiers in Neuroscience. 18(9), 2015:55. doi:10.3389/fnins.2015.00055.
         "Price points out that the first mammals were often preyed on by reptiles and birds and consequently the mammalian brain evolved to enable quick instinctive reactions (Price, 2005). Immediate threat responses were, and continue to be, hard-wired spinal reflexes that provide rapid reactions to threat (Lee et al., 1996)."
     https://www.ncbi.nlm.nih.gov/pmc/articles/PMC4364301.
         Price Joseph L. "Free Will Versus Survival: Brain Systems that Underlie Intrinsic Constraints on Behavior." Journal of Comparative Neurology. 493(1), 2005: 132–9. doi: 10.1002/cne.20750. https://pubmed.ncbi.nlm.nih.gov/16255003.
4   Bruno S. Frey, David A. Savage, & Benno Torgler. "Interaction of Natural Survival Instincts and Internalized Social Norms Exploring the Titanic and Lusitania Disasters." PNAS. 107(11), 2010: 4862–65. https://doi.org/10.1073/pnas.0911303107.

While these instincts are about survival, the first is concerned with *immediate* survival, and the second are related to long-term survival.

For this reason, when a person feels safe (which means loved, respected, and abundant, in addition to being physically safe) their automatic instinct is to reach out and help others. That's built in as part of how the human brain works[5, 6].

If a person does *not* automatically feel a desire to help others, be kind, compassionate, and share, it's because their brain is in survival mode[7]. Bearing in mind that, to the unconscious part of the brain, survival equates to feeling loved, respected, valued, and abundant (*"If the tribe doesn't love, respect, and value me, I'll be rejected and die,"* and *"If I don't get enough, I'll die"*), it is logical that all negative emotional states put the brain and body into that state of emergency.

Regardless of the *reality* of their circumstances, this is all about how a person feels—based on their implicit childhood memories. Even if they're wealthy; even if they are loved and respected by others; even if they're powerful and successful in their field, if their brain repeatedly refers to "evidence" from their childhood experiences that "proves" they're in danger because they're *not* loved and *not* valued, it will still be putting them into that state of immediate survival, regardless of their current reality.

Remember, helping others is *secondary* to immediate survival.

While changing the way children are raised is an essential part of changing our world, what we'll share in this book is that those changes can also be made *retroactively*.

5   Abigail A. Marsh. "Neural, Cognitive, and Evolutionary Foundations of Human Altruism." WIREs Wiley Interdisciplinary Reviews: Cognitive Science, 7(1), 2016: 59–71. doi/10.1002/wcs.1377.

6   University of California, Los Angeles. "Your Brain Might be Hard-wired for Altruism: Neuroscience Research Suggests an Avenue for Treating the Empathically Challenged." ScienceDaily. March 18, 2016. www.sciencedaily.com/releases/2016/03/160318102101.htm.

7   University of Zurich. "The Evolutionary Roots of Human Altruism." ScienceDaily. August 27, 2014. www.sciencedaily.com/releases/2014/08/140827092002.htm.

Blame

This is not about blaming those who raised us. If they had been raised differently—with kindness, compassion, love, affection, support, respect, freedom, enthusiasm, encouragement, fun, and feelings of being safe—they would have become different adults. They would have become different parents and grandparents. They would have automatically treated us in the same way they were treated as children. This doesn't excuse what happened to you. There is no excuse, and all children deserve kindness, love, compassion, support, and affection; all children deserve to feel safe and loved unconditionally. Recognizing that their childhood determined their self-image, worldview, beliefs, and behaviors is not about excusing them, it's about empowering *you*. Blame doesn't empower. And this is all about self-empowerment.

We consider this information to be fundamental in improving world problems. From environmental solutions to peace among nations, to transforming communities, and solving poverty, discrimination, and derision—our goal is to help individuals to automatically feel safe, happy, and loved because their brains are referring to new "evidence" that "proves" their new empowered self-image and worldview.

The knock-on effects will be the secondary human priorities: connection, kindness, compassion, and finding solutions based on those qualities.

It starts inside the individual.

Community and Connection

We have worked with hundreds of people using our methods. The information we share in this book will empower you too to change your *own* negative childhood memories to the opposite, positive, and empowering. Having said that, it's important to know you're not alone. As Dr. Bruce Perry and Oprah Winfrey explain in their book, *What Happened to You?* a supportive community is a key component of effectively healing from childhood trauma—though there doesn't necessarily need to have been trauma for you to need that support. Whether it's your church, a club, family, or a group of good friends, if you feel safe and supported with them, ask for help and connection as you need it. We have a loving, supportive community[8] that you're very welcome to join as well. We would love to hear from you!

We've included a Frequently Asked Questions section at the end of the book, but if the answer to your question isn't there, please feel free to reach out to us through our website or social media. We're here for you!

A Note on Trauma

It's important that you do not attempt to address trauma on your own.

Trauma is experienced differently by different people, and through our work with clients, we've found that trauma is not always what most people expect it to be. Regardless of the events themselves, if a memory feels highly triggering, we recommend asking for help with it. If, when you consider a particular event, the negative feelings are an 8 or higher, on a scale of 1 to 10, where 10 is the most triggering, we recommend you contact a certified Remmert Method practitioner (you can find a list of practitioners trained and certified by us, on our website). You can also seek support with changing your traumatic memories by joining one of our private group sessions or workshops (we can help you to change the memories without your needing to share any details) or by contacting us for guidance via social media.

Sensitive Topics

We share some emotionally sensitive topics in this book, including suicidal state of mind. Although we don't go into any unnecessary detail, and all the experiences we share have happy endings, some readers may find the subjects themselves triggering. Do keep reading (reaching out to us if you need support as you go), because these examples and stories are a key part of empowering you and freeing you from those triggers.

---

8 "The Remmert Method." www.facebook.com/groups/theremmertmethod/

If you or someone you know is at risk of suicide, please call the National Suicide Prevention Lifeline at 800-273-8255, text -HOME to 741741, or visit SpeakingOfSuicide.com/resources.

Real-Life Examples

This book is a collaboration, and while most of it is written, jointly, by both of us, you'll hear from us separately as we talk about our own individual stories.

We also share experiences from some of our clients and those in our community. We've changed their names and identifying information to protect their privacy.

A Word for Parents

We are both parents ourselves and we know that learning this information can be a double-edged sword. As you find out about the effects of your own childhood on your life as an adult, and learn to change those negative memories, you may find your mind wandering to your parenting of your own children. Depending on what references your brain holds from your childhood, this can be a strong trigger for guilt and regret. We've both been there! It's important to remind yourself, as you go through this book, that you have done the best you could with the childhood references you had at the time. We are all children in adult bodies, trying to cope with adult responsibilities. Think of it this way: Considering that all our coping skills are learned in childhood, it is effectively the child in you who has been trying to parent your children. How can a child be blamed for not being able to parent effectively?

You are always—unconsciously—doing the best you can with what you have. And the key to empowering your children, moving forward (whether they're still children or not), is to first address your own references. You can't give what you don't have. So, keep your focus on changing your own childhood memories, and the positive knock-on effects on your relationship with your children will be automatic.

The most effective way you can empower your own child is to change the childhood of their parent—you. If your parents had had different childhood experiences—if they had felt safe and loved throughout their childhood—they would have been different parents to you. They would have made different choices, and they would have automatically treated you the same way they were treated—with kindness, compassion, respect, support, enthusiasm, and patience. The same goes for you. If you had had that kind of childhood, yourself, you would have automatically been a different parent to your own children. But now you can make that change, moving forward. You can't go back in time and change how you've parented your children up until now, but you can change your relationship with them, automatically, from this moment onward, by changing your own childhood memories.

It starts with you.

Note From the Authors

Think of the changes you want to make in your life—whatever they are—as a destination.

This book is designed to take you from where you are now to that destination. Whether that is peace of mind, feeling happier, being in a loving relationship, feeling confident and safe, feeling loved and connected, improving your financial situation, improving your physical or mental health, or changing anything else about your life or yourself, the way to get there is by learning to drive your vehicle, setting the GPS coordinates to match that desired destination, and then staying on the road until you reach it.

We are so excited for you!

The End

by Odille

It was early evening. I sat in my car in the empty parking lot of the local library and tightened my grip on the steering wheel. The library was closed on Wednesdays, and I was alone. I stared at the brick wall several yards in front of me and revved the engine. I had thought about suicide many times throughout my life, but this was the closest I had come to going through with it. And I was going to do it by driving my car into a brick wall. All I had to do was release the handbrake and put my foot flat to the floor. It would be over before I knew it.

I remember that feeling well. Part of what we'll share in this book is why, at the time I was in that emotional state, ending my life by driving into that brick wall seemed like a good idea. And why no logic or reasoning could have made a difference to that decision.

What I didn't know back then are three simple but revolutionary facts:

1. Thoughts are connections between neurons[9] (nerve cells) in the neocortex of the brain, and those connections trigger matching chemicals: Positive thoughts trigger "feel-good" chemicals, and negative thoughts trigger stress chemicals.

---

9   John H. Byrne. "Introduction to Neurons and Neuronal Networks." Neuroscience Online. October 10, 2021. https://nba.uth.tmc.edu/neuroscience/m/s1/introduction.html.

2. Stress chemicals cause blood to drain from the prefrontal cortex of the brain[10] (where we do our cognitive thinking).

3. Implicit childhood memories provide the "evidence" that "proves" our self-image and worldview[11]. In turn, our self-image and world-view provide the foundation for our unconscious decisions and actions. And those memories can be changed to the opposite, positive, and empowering[12]!

When we're feeling any negative emotion, the stress chemicals that create these emotions cause blood to drain from the prefrontal cortex (where we do our cognitive thinking) to the back of the brain. This is part of our survival system (fight-flight-freeze). When we're faced with immediate physical threat, the priority is to escape—by running away, fighting, or shutting down. These instinctive responses are controlled by the brain stem. Since the time it takes us to think consciously could cost us our life, we automatically switch to using our built-in, unconscious survival instinct. This means that whenever we're feeling intense negative emotions, we quite literally can't think straight because we don't have access to that part of the brain.

You may have noticed that when you've been emotionally triggered in an encounter with someone, it's only later that you think of all the things you should, or could, have said. While you were in the middle of the situation and experiencing those intense emotions, your prefrontal cortex was "offline." Later, as the level of stress chemicals in your system lowered, and blood started to return to that part of your brain, it allowed you to think more clearly.

This is one of the main reasons that, from that intense, painful emotional state, killing myself by driving into a brick wall seemed to make

---

10 Amy F. T. Arnsten. "Stress Signalling Pathways that Impair Prefrontal Cortex Structure and Function." Nature Reviews Neuroscience. 10(6), 2009: 410–22. doi:10.1038/nrn2648

11 "Implicit Memory." ScienceDirect. https://www.sciencedirect.com/topics/social-sciences/implicit-memory.

12 Jonathan L. C. Lee, Karim Nader, & Daniela Schiller. "An Update on Memory Reconsolidation Updating." Trends in Cognitive Sciences. 21(7), 2017: 531–45. doi:10.1016/j.tics.2017.04.006.

sense. The part of my brain that was able to use logic and reason, problem solve, and see consequences was offline. Those stress chemicals had created the same state of emergency they would if I were faced with a bear. When faced with a bear, there is no time to think strategically or negotiate—we must act instinctively and immediately and that's what the back of the brain enables us to do.

Unfortunately, because that unconscious part of the brain has no ability to reason or use logic, it also can't distinguish between immediate physical threat and emotional pain—or between reality and imagination[13]. The same chemicals (creating the same physiological effect) are in play in all those scenarios. Blood drains from the prefrontal cortex whether we're in immediate physical danger, thinking about something we're worried about, or feeling betrayed by a loved one.

Not everyone has been suicidal. But everyone has experienced emotional pain. How we navigate those painful experiences, circumstances, and events is determined, not by our conscious efforts, but by the implicit memories created through childhood experiences—the memories that provide the brain with references that "prove" who we are and how the world works[14].

As you notice that it's raining outside, your brain refers to unconscious memory that provides information on what rain is, whether it's dangerous or not, and any other relevant data. That information is not based on objective facts regarding the rain itself. Rather, it's based on your childhood experiences of rain. For example, you automatically know, without thinking about it, that if you walk out into the rain, you'll get wet. You probably can't remember the first time you learned about rain through experience, but your brain has the information stored (implicit memory) so that you're able to react automatically.

13   University of Colorado at Boulder. "Your Brain on Imagination: It's A Lot Like Reality, Study Shows." ScienceDaily. December 10, 2018. www.sciencedaily.com/releases/2018/12/181210144943.htm.

14   Marianne E. Lloyd & Jeremy Miller. APA Psychnet. In P. J. Bauer & R. Fivush (Eds). The Wiley Handbook on the Development of Children's Memory (pp. 336–59). (Hoboken, NJ: Wiley Blackwell). https://psycnet.apa.org/record/2013-26762-015.

You may also notice that you have an emotional response—which may be different from someone else's. One person may see the rain and immediately feel a desire to walk in it. Someone else may see the rain and feel grateful. Another may see the rain and immediately feel sad, or annoyed. What creates the difference between these automatic responses is the references from each person's past that the brain is referring to that determine not only what rain is, but what it means and how to respond to it. And all without our conscious awareness.

Implicit memories are based on experience, not on fact.

Formed primarily in childhood, they provide the "evidence" that "proves" our core beliefs—*whether those beliefs are true or not*[15].

This is why efforts by the conscious mind to improve self-esteem and confidence, how we relate to others, and even how we manage money, aren't always effective. Because no matter how much we may want to change, and no matter what we do to try to change, the unconscious part of the brain is still referring to those references from childhood that *prove* our current beliefs and behavior patterns.

Just like a GPS that's still set for the previous destination, whenever we venture too far from familiar patterns and experiences (no matter how unwanted those experiences may be), the unconscious part of the brain "corrects" the course. Some may call it self-sabotage, but it's really no more self-sabotage than a GPS is capable of sabotage. In the same way, if your printer prints in red ink, and you want the documents in blue you need to change the ink cartridge from red to blue. The printer is not sabotaging your print job, it just prints documents using what it has—it's automatic.

Regardless of how hard I had previously tried to change my patterns

15   Henry Otgaar, Alan Scoboria, & Tom Smeets. "Experimentally Evoking Nonbelieved Memories for Childhood Events," Journal of Experimental Psychology: Learning, Memory, and Cognition. 39(3), 2013: 717–30. https://doi.org/10.1037/a0029668

of emotional, physical, and financial struggle, my brain would repeat edly make sure that the course was "corrected" back to my unbearable normal.

Pointless

As I sat in my car that evening, feeling the compulsion to put my foot down and release the handbrake, I had no idea of what was going on in my brain. It would be years before I learned how the brain works, before I had the tools that we'll be sharing with you in this book.

I was drained from the gut-wrenching sobbing, and now I felt quite calm and determined. This was definitely best, for everyone. It wasn't failure in itself, it wasn't my financial problems, it wasn't the fibromyalgia or the IBS, it wasn't that my life had turned out completely differently to what I had hoped. It was the fact that there was no hope now.

Having failed financially, yet again, despite working so hard, the realization had come to me that regardless of what I did, what choices I made, how hard I worked, how many times I pulled myself up and tried again, I wasn't meant to succeed. What if this was just the way my "story" was written? What if I was like a character in a video game, who just wanted a quiet, peaceful, happy life, but the "player" had other plans?

That was the only logical explanation for me: No matter what I did or how hard I tried, my life was never going to improve—*I* was never going to improve—because that wasn't my story. I felt like a little child trying to punch the adult, who's effortlessly keeping the child at arm's length with his hand on her forehead.

It was pointless.

It was just more rounds of getting-up-and-falling-down-and-getting-up-and-falling-down…and I didn't want to get up anymore. It was the latest, and lowest point, in my yoyo existence of putting my heart and soul into working hard, and being knocked down, yet again.

I revved the engine, and was about to release the handbrake, when my phone rang. I glanced at it, lying on the passenger seat beside me. It was my sister. There was no way I would answer it because I knew she would talk me out of what I planned to do. And I knew there was no point in that. I also knew there was absolutely no point in talking about anything. I was sick of talking about it. I was sick of thinking about it. I felt that even if I tried to talk, nothing would come out of my mouth. There was nothing left to say. There was nothing left in me. There was no point in even trying. Anything.

The call went to voicemail. I looked at the brick wall again. This was definitely the best option. My sister would be better off without me. My mother and brother would be better off without me. And my son would be better off without me. Once I was gone, they would all be able to move on and live happy lives. I would no longer be a financial burden on my sister, and my son would be raised by someone with better financial stability. I thought of my son, spending that evening with friends. He had his whole life ahead of him, and he would get the support he would need, without me as a weight around his ankles.

I love my son more than anything. He has always been the most important thing in the world to me. I would do anything for him. If I didn't know what I now know about the brain, none of it would make sense. From outside of that intensely painful emotional state, my mind would go to the horrific impact my suicide would have on my family—especially my son. But, looking back on my state of mind on that day from where I am now, with my knowledge of how the brain works, it all makes perfect sense.

I had spent my life being "good." Following instructions, following directions, doing as I was told, and yet I was still struggling. I had been the "good little girl," but I was still being punished. I thought of myself as far from a victim as you can get—I worked hard, was constantly looking for solutions, and was willing to do what needed to be done…if only I knew what that was.

What I didn't realize at the time is that I was in a different type of victim mindset. I was still the child, trying to be good so that she would be safe. My perception, and worldview, was still: *If I do the right things, something or someone outside of me will be pleased, and I will be rewarded.*

My work ethic, drive to please, and compulsion to keep trying was based on my implicit childhood memories that "proved" that this is who I am and how the world works. The references from my childhood provided the unconscious "evidence" of the following: Life, for me, is a constant struggle that never results in reward, and I come from a long line of people who struggled without reward.

I'd been through every self-development and financial improvement method, modality, and belief system I could find. I had done all the things. I'd followed Tony Robbins and thrown myself into "massive action."[16] I'd read *Rich Dad, Poor Dad*[17] and completely changed my beliefs about money. I had worked extra jobs, budgeted, sacrificed, and prayed. I had followed financial and business advice to the letter. I'd been positive. I'd done the hours of visualization—imagining in present tense, with feeling. I had done the affirmations—in present tense, with feeling. I had reached out for help on forums. I had done Louise Hay's "mirror work"[18] and I had followed Neville Goddard's advice. I had done the "energy work" and spiritual exploration. I had used self-hypnosis and subliminal messaging and received regular psychotherapy.

Every single time, I had fully believed that I'd found the solution, and I committed to it with all my heart. And every time I would eventually find myself back in the state of struggle. When I did make some extra money, my car would break down, I would get ill, someone wouldn't pay me—something would always happen to get me back into that quagmire.

---

16   Tony Robbins. "How To Make a Massive Action Plan (MAP)." Tony Robbins. Accessed on October 11, 2021. https://www.tonyrobbins.com/career-business/how-to-make-a-massive-action-plan-map/.

17   Robert Kiyosaki and Sharon L. Lechter. (2000). "Rich Dad, Poor Dad." (Warner Books)

18   Louise Hay. "What Is Mirror Work." Louise Hay. Accessed on October 11, 2021. https://www.louisehay.com/what-is-mirror-work.

The phone rang again. My sister—again. I watched her name on the screen as the phone rang until it went to voicemail. Then, a text. I didn't open it. There was no point. Another call. I still didn't answer, but then a memory came into my mind of my sister telling me about her own suicidal thoughts and plans.

My Sister's Suicide Plan

I clearly remembered her telling me about the agreement she'd made with herself. That when she felt the urge to kill herself, she would agree to do it, but she would do it later. She'd found that the compulsion was so strong that trying *not* to do it wouldn't make a difference. If anything, her mind would come up with increasingly convincing reasons for following through with it. Instead, she would decide she would go ahead, but that there was no rush. If it really was the best option, then that wouldn't change in the next few hours. Having made the decision, she would watch soccer on TV first, and then, if she still wanted to do it later that day or tomorrow, she would. She had no interest in soccer and didn't really know much about it, but through experience she had found that, for some reason, watching soccer on TV with the sound down, was soothing for her. So, by the time "later" or tomorrow came, the overwhelming urge to kill herself had subsided enough for her not to want to go through with it.

That memory of my sister sharing her strategy was enough to break through the immediate urgency to end my own life. It was enough to change my emotional state from suicidal to what felt like a deeper sense of surrender. Surrender to nothing. Not even the action of ending my life. Surrender to just sitting. I turned off the engine and just sat, staring at the brick wall. I don't know how long I sat, staring, but at some point, the next decision came to me. I would just exist. I wasn't going to try anymore. I would just exist.

That was May 21st, 2008. I remember the date because it was the day before my son's 12th birthday. Once I had come out of that emotional pit, I couldn't believe that I was capable of even considering doing that to my child—what a horrific thing to inflict on him at all, but especially the unthinkable timing that would have forever connected that pain to his birthday. I felt like Jekyll and Hyde—I didn't recognize the me that had sat in that car.

Although I never again came that close to taking my life, the physical, emotional, and financial struggle continued. And despite my decision that evening, to "just exist," my relentless optimism and drive to improve kicked in, and I continued to try. I resumed that old pattern of getting excited and enthusiastic about finding a solution, putting my heart and soul into it, and failing. Over, and over again.

I kept searching for solutions, trying everything I came across, from Esther Hicks' Law of Attraction[19] to borrowing money so that, in April 2014, I could sign up with a one-to-one business coach who had an excellent track record of helping entrepreneurs create successful businesses. Despite my diligence in following his advice and working harder than most, I failed again. Against all odds.

I'd like to say it was a journey, and that each step contributed to where I am today, but the truth is, those years were more like wandering around in the wilderness, unable to navigate back to the road. Some of the (too many to count) paths I explored in my attempts to find my way during those years included:

- Applying for different jobs
- Financial saving strategies
- Rhonda Byrne's *The Secret*[20]
- Self-help forums
- Various low-paying jobs
- Home businesses

---

19   Esther Hicks. (2005). The Law of Attraction: The Basics of the Teachings of Abraham. (Carlsbad, CA: Hay House Inc.).

20   Rhonda Byrne. (2008). The Secret. (London: Simon & Schuster).

- EFT (Emotional Freedom Technique)[21]
- Ho'oponopono
- Reiki
- Flotation tanks
- Past life regression
- Crystal healing
- Various energy healing
- Learning from Joe Dispenza[22], Bruce Lipton[23], Bob Proctor[24], and Gregg Braden[25]
- Abraham–Hicks and the Law of Attraction
- Mike Dooley's The Universe Talks[26]
- *What the Bleep do We Know?*[27]
- Integrative psychotherapy
- Affirmations
- Visualization
- Self-hypnosis
- Subliminal messaging
- Binaural beats
- The Silva Method[28]
- Joseph Murphy's *The Power of Your Subconscious Mind*[29]
- Various meditation methods
- Buddhism
- Psych-K®[30]
- Various methods of budgeting
- Following the advice of a financial advisor
- Too many books to mention

---

21   Gary Craig. "EFT." www.emofree.com/.
22   Dr. Joe Dispenza. https://drjoedispenza.com/.
23   Bruce Lipton Ph.D. https://www.brucelipton.com/.
24   Bob Proctor. https://www.proctorgallagherinstitute.com/.
25   Gregg Braden. https://www.greggbraden.com/.
26   Mike Dooley. The Universe Talks. https://www.tut.com/.
27   William Arntz, Betsy Chasse, Mark Vicente, dirs. What the Bleep Do We Know? (2004; Phoenix: Roadside Attraction & Samuel Goldwyn Films, 2004), documentary.
28   Jose Silva. (1991). The Silva Mind Control Method. (New York, NY: Pocket Books).
29   Joseph Murphy. The Power of Your Subconscious Mind. (Merchant Books, 2019).
30   Rob Williams. (2004). PSYCH-K…The Missing Piece/Peace in Your Life. 2nd edition. (Myrddin Publications).

Despite all these methods, which I'd seen had been so effective for others, there seemed to be something fundamentally wrong with *me*. I spent almost eight years trying and failing, on an emotional rollercoaster of getting excited that I'd found the solution, and then plummeting into the depths of despair again. By June 2015, I was 51 years old, alone, renting a room in a shared house, cleaning other people's houses, and still unable to pay my bills.

It was toward the end of 2015 that I finally came across Robert G. Smith's videos on YouTube. Robert had created the methodology FasterEFT™[31] and, although I'd tried EFT (Emotional Freedom Technique) in the past, this was different. As I watched Robert's presentation on the effects of negative childhood memories on the adult, I realized that *that* was the missing piece! Based on what I'd learned about the brain up to that point, it made perfect sense to me. Robert went on to demonstrate how those memories could be changed. I binge-watched his videos, absorbing as much as I could, and then tried his method out for myself. Although Steve and I have developed, and added to, our own method of changing childhood memories—which we will take you through, step-by-step, in Chapter 5—I first started changing my negative childhood memories using FasterEFT, following Robert's videos and training.

At last, I began to see significant changes, both in myself and, as a result, in my circumstances. One morning, about a week after starting to change my negative childhood memories, I woke up thinking differently! I found myself coming up with solutions and options that I realized would probably seem obvious to others, but that I had never thought of before! More on those later.

Within a few months, not only was I able to pay my bills, but I was also traveling internationally and paying for my son and my sister to join me on a trip to Greece—on May 21st, 2016. It was my birthday present to my son, and an early one for my sister's June birthday. The brick wall from

---

31   Robert G. Smith "FasterEFT." www.fastereft.com.

exactly eight years earlier didn't even enter my mind at that time, and I've only just realized the synchronicity, as I'm writing this. Eight years, to the day. From the worst thing I could have done to them for their birthdays, to a present that was not only fun, exciting, and full of non-stop laughter together, but that I was able to pay for on my own. By October 2019, I owned three of the rental properties I used to clean back in 2015.

I had changed my brain's GPS coordinates (my negative implicit childhood memories) from struggle and pain to love, joy, safety, abundance, empowerment, and connection. And the results had been automatic. I started thinking differently, noticed different opportunities, made different decisions, and identified different solutions. My perception, judgment, creativity, communication, and risk-assessment had completely changed. All automatically.

Steve and I turned those processes into the Three Pillars of The Remmert Method:

- Pillar One: Learning to Drive—Changing Your Brain and Body Chemistry
- Pillar Two: Changing the GPS—Childhood Memory Transformation (CMT)
- Pillar Three: Staying on the Road—Zero Tolerance

Everything else I'd tried up until then had only succeeded in cutting off the branches and leaves of the weeds in my life. Now I'd found out how to pull those weeds out by the roots, plant the seeds of the flowers I wanted, and water those flowers until my garden was filled with them. And I'm so excited to be sharing that method and those techniques with you here, so that you have the power to do the same for your own life!

RECAP:

- Thoughts are connections between neurons (nerve cells) in the neocortex of the brain.

- Those connections trigger matching chemicals that cause sensations that we experience as feelings.
- Stress chemicals triggered by negative thoughts cause blood to drain from the prefrontal cortex of the brain which means we lose access to our cognitive-thinking ability.
- Implicit (unconscious) childhood memories provide the "evidence" that "proves" our self-image and worldview and, in turn, determine our automatic perceptions, responses, behaviors, and reactions.
- Those memories can be changed to the opposite, positive, and empowering.
- The unconscious part of the brain will now refer to the new implicit childhood memories as "fact" while we are still able to consciously recall what originally happened (explicit memory).
- Changing negative childhood memories to the opposite, positive, and empowering results in automatic changes in our self-image and worldview, which determines new experiences in life, moving forward.

Pillar One

LEARNING TO DRIVE—CHANGING YOUR BRAIN AND BODY CHEMISTRY

You Can Control Your Own Brain Chemistry

If you wanted to drive from the city to the beach, and you didn't know how to drive, you probably wouldn't get very far. Learning to drive the vehicle first is, of course, essential to being able to get to your end destination. You wouldn't need to know all the details of how the vehicle works—although, if you're interested in those mechanics, you might voluntarily learn that information—but you'd need to know the basics, in order to understand how to operate that vehicle.

In the same way, knowing the basics of the biology that results in how you feel, and how to "drive" your brain and body, is essential in successfully making the changes you want to make in your life.

> *"Emotional warmth produces the hormone oxytocin in the brain and throughout the body. Of much recent interest is its significant role in the cardiovascular system."*
> —David R. Hamilton Ph.D.[32]

We had a client (we'll call her Alice) in 2017, who had been working

---

32   David R. Hamilton. "5 Beneficial Side Effects of Kindness." HuffPost. Updated August 2, 2011. https://www.huffpost.com/entry/kindness-benefits_b_869537.

on herself for a few years. However, she found she was still triggered by certain experiences with other people. She found it impossible to avoid feeling hurt and angry when a loved one didn't reply to her messages. Despite all the work she'd done to improve herself, she was still at the mercy of the actions (or inaction) of others.

Over time, Alice developed the skill of controlling her own brain chemistry, using the technique we'll share with you. She found that she was being triggered less and less frequently, and when she was upset, she was able to get through it much quicker. This had a knock-on effect on her relationships—she was able to communicate with others more effectively and ask for what she wanted in a strategic and straightforward way, rather than being driven by negative emotions.

The great news is that all the basics you need to know to control your own brain chemistry are no more complicated than the basics you need to drive a car.

In a nutshell: Connections between neurons (thoughts) trigger chemicals that determine not only how we're feeling, but whether we have access to the cognitive-thinking part of our brains or not.

By developing the skill of controlling our brain chemistry, we control how we feel, as well as our ability to problem-solve and think strategically.

Because the stress chemicals produced when we're in a negative emotional state cause blood to drain from the prefrontal cortex (where we do our cognitive thinking), we literally don't have access to the part of the brain we need for thinking clearly. Trying to problem-solve, process information, communicate effectively, be creative, think of alternative options, and assess risk while we are triggered emotionally is like trying to drive with the handbrake on.

So, for example, when Alice sent a text and didn't receive a reply within a certain timeframe, her brain automatically triggered stress chemicals based on her childhood experiences of being abandoned and ignored (which we'll go into in more detail in the next chapter), and those stress chemicals created sensations in her body: pressure in her chest, an increase in her heart rate, and a slight tightening of her throat.

The moment she became aware of those feelings, Alice's conscious mind automatically interpreted those sensations as "hurt." Since the conscious mind's job is to make sense of experiences, it automatically and instantly focused on the *apparent* reasons for the hurt that were in front of her in that moment. When those neurons connected, they triggered yet more stress chemicals. And when she thought about the fact that the person didn't respond to her, and therefore didn't care, those thoughts led to *"no one cares"* —in other words, more "evidence" she's unworthy and unloved—and so those feelings were perpetuated.

As that cycle of stress chemicals (feelings of being ignored and being hurt) and the specific connections between neurons (thoughts about all the apparent reasons why no one cares about her, and what that means) continued to build, blood drained from the cognitive-thinking part of Alice's brain, and she was unable to think rationally. Caught in the loop of emotional pain and the thoughts that maintained the momentum of that pain, Alice was unable to see anything outside of it.

She was unable to reason that the person may not have received the text or may be very busy, and that their lack of response didn't have anything to do with her. She was unable to come up with the words that would let the person know what she needed. That part of her brain was offline. She became stuck in the mud. And the more she tried to think about it, the faster those wheels spun.

While this process in the brain is on automatic by default, there is a simple little exercise that we taught Alice and will also share with you, that will empower you to gain control over your brain chemistry, as well as condition your brain and body to produce lower levels of stress chemicals and higher levels of "feel-good" chemicals over time. Just like getting physically fit.

Under the Hood: What You First Need to Know

Thoughts are connections between neurons in the neocortex of the brain. Those connections trigger matching chemicals and those chemicals create feelings. To put it simply: Negative thoughts trigger stress chemicals; positive thoughts trigger "feel-good" chemicals.

Since all negative emotions fall at a level somewhere in the fight-flight-freeze emergency state, whenever you're feeling a negative emotion, your brain and body will be producing stress chemicals[33].

That means that your brain and body are going into the same state they would if you were faced with immediate physical danger. Some effects of those stress chemicals on the system are:

- Blood is pumped away from the organs to the extremities[34] (for running away or fighting)
- Blood drains from the prefrontal cortex (where we do our cognitive thinking) to the back of the brain (the unconscious part)—because, when we're faced with a bear, there's no time to negotiate, strategize, or problem-solve; we need to take immediate, instinctive action if we want to survive

The result is that negative emotions are about more than just feeling bad—they mean we literally can't think straight! This is why, after we calm down from being triggered, we think of all the things we should have said in the moment.

The stress chemicals that were causing Alice's feelings of being ignored and hurt were part of the same survival system that would have been triggered if she'd been in immediate physical danger.

---

33   Lou Whitaker. "How Does Thinking Positive Thoughts Affect Neuroplasticity?" Meteor Education. https://meteoreducation.com/how-does-thinking-positive-thoughts-affect-neuroplasticity/ accessed October 10, 2021.

34   Brianna Chu, Komal Marwaha, Terrence Sanvictores, & Derek Ayers. "Physiology, Stress Reaction." StatPearls. (2021). https://www.ncbi.nlm.nih.gov/books/NBK541120

All of this is perfectly normal and healthy—short-term. The problem comes when we are living in these stressed states for prolonged periods of time.

In addition to the chemical response to the connections between neurons as we think consciously, there is also a chemical response to input from sensory receptors. In other words, as we experience the world around us—as we see, hear, smell, taste, and feel—the brain automatically refers to the information it holds from our previous experiences of that sensation, and then automatically prompts a chemical response[35]. For example: An expression on someone's face matches a parent's expression and automatically triggers a cocktail of stress chemicals.

Those chemicals create sensations and emotions (fear, anger, anxiety, confusion) without our conscious engagement or awareness.

We then consciously give meaning to those sensations and emotions (*I'm not good enough, they don't like me*). And as those neurons connect, they produce yet more of the same stress chemicals. You can see how this process is perpetuated and continues to confirm those negative beliefs, self-image, and experience of the world around us.

How to Drive: Controlling Your Own Brain Chemistry

It is possible to change your own chemistry from stress chemicals to "feel-good" chemicals—as long as you keep your focus off the negative and on the positive, for between 60 and 90 seconds.

As neuroscientist Jill Bolte Taylor[36] explains in her concept of the "90-Second Rule," it takes under 90 seconds from the point of a trigger for the peak and dissipation of stress chemicals. During those 60 to 90 seconds, the stress chemicals dissipate, flushing through your system, and

---

35   Joseph E. LeDoux & Richard Brown. "A Higher-Order Theory of Emotional Consciousness." PNAS. 114(10), 2017: E2016–25. https://doi.org/10.1073/pnas.1619316114.
36   Jill Bolte Taylor. (2009). My Stroke of Insight. (London: Hodder).

allowing your brain and body to return to a calm state—unless, that is, they are retriggered.

So, for example, as you think about something you're worried about, those connections between neurons (thoughts) trigger the release of stress chemicals into your system. You'll feel the effects of those chemicals in the form of worry or anxiety.

If you were to stop there and create different neural connections (by thinking thoughts that aren't worrying), you would no longer feel the effects of those stress chemicals, and the worry or anxiety would be gone. Of course, what happens for most of us, automatically and naturally, is this: We have feelings of worry, we automatically think about them, and we automatically think of all the reasons for those fears. And each neural connection (thought) triggers a new burst of stress chemicals, restarting that 90-second clock each time.

While you're focusing on what triggers you, you are pumping stress chemicals into your system, in real time. Just like leaving the hot water tap running will fill the bath with hot water. As long as you switch that hot water tap off and keep the cold water tap running instead, you are changing the temperature of the water. Of course, if you switch the cold water tap off and switch the hot water tap back on, you'll end up with a very hot bath again.

In the same way, those "taps" are connections between neurons in the neocortex of your brain. The "hot water tap" represents connections between neurons as you think about things that trigger you—things you're worried about, things that hurt you, things that make you angry, anything that doesn't feel good. The "cold water tap" represents connections between neurons as you think about things that feel good—things you love, things you're grateful for, things you're looking forward to, anything that feels good.

Keep that "stress chemical tap" off, and that "feel-good chemical tap" running for a minute and a half, and you'll have changed your brain and body chemistry from stress chemicals to "feel-good" chemicals.

It's Not What it Looks Like!

Imagine someone who has never experienced electricity before. They walk into a room with an overhead light in the center of the ceiling. At first, the light is off, then the lightbulb lights up, then it goes off again. Since they've never encountered electricity before, they don't know that the way to make that lightbulb light up is to flick the switch on the wall—they'd focus on the lightbulb itself. They'd try to figure out how to make the light come on by fully focusing on that lightbulb.

Of course, there's no visible connection between the lightbulb and the switch on the wall behind them. But *you* know that in order to make the lightbulb light up you need to take your focus off the lightbulb (perhaps even turn your back on it if the switch is behind you) and flick the switch on the wall. Flicking that switch results in the lightbulb being illuminated in the center of the room.

The lightbulb represents how you're feeling. The switch represents the connections between neurons (thoughts) that trigger the chemical reaction that results in the way you're feeling. In order to change how you feel, you need to take your focus off the feelings (the lightbulb) and *choose* what your focus will be (flicking the switch).

Take a moment, right now, to test this for yourself.

Take a deep breath, close your eyes, and think of your favorite color. If you don't have a favorite, just pick one you like. Imagine being surrounded by that beautiful color. Allow yourself to experience the feeling of that color and notice what you love about it. Fully focus on it. Notice how you feel. What you're feeling is the effect of "feel-good" chemicals.

Now think about something or someone you're worried about—just briefly—and notice the difference in how you feel. What you're feeling now is the effect of stress chemicals.

Now go back to thinking about your favorite color. Again, imagine being surrounded by that beautiful color. Allow yourself to fully focus on what you love about it. Notice how you feel.

The "switch" on the wall is your focus. The current setting of that switch determines the state of the lightbulb in the center of the room. Your focus (the neural connections you're making at a particular moment) determines what chemicals your brain and body are producing—which determines how you're feeling.

It's simple, but not easy. Change your focus from negative to positive and you change your brain chemistry from stress chemicals to "feel-good" chemicals, which, in turn, changes how you feel and how you think. The reason it's not easy is because stress chemicals are stronger than "feel-good" chemicals—after all, stress chemicals create our survival response[37]. It's more important to focus on the wild animal that's threatening to attack us than on the pretty flowers!

Stress chemicals are designed to get—and keep—our attention on the "danger" until that danger has gone. It's all about survival.

The problem is that the part of the brain that triggers that emergency response can't tell the difference between an immediate physical threat and the "danger" of someone judging us, or the memory of a mean comment, or any other negative emotional experience[38]. This is why it's easier to feel bad than to feel good.

37   David S. Goldstein. "Adrenal Responses to Stress." Cellular and Molecular Neurobiology. 30(8), 2010:1433–40. doi:10.1007/s10571-010-9606-9 https://www.ncbi.nlm.nih.gov/pmc/articles/PMC3056281.

38   Samuel T. Moulton & Stephen M. Kosslyn. "Imagining Predictions: Mental Imagery as Mental Emulation." Philos Trans R Soc Lond B Biol Sci. 364(1521), 2009:1273–80. doi: 10.1098/rstb.2008.0314.
       https://pubmed.ncbi.nlm.nih.gov/19528008.

It's a Skill

Gaining control over your brain chemistry is a skill. Just like learning a musical instrument, or any other physical skill. With practice, it becomes easier.

At first, when Alice waited for a response to her text, and didn't get one, the feelings of being ignored and hurt were instant and intense. That was the effect of the stress chemicals in her system—her brain and body had already gone into that emergency state before she became consciously aware of it. It was impossible for her to switch her focus to something positive (even just her favorite color) from the middle of that triggered state, with her body full of stress chemicals.

However, as she practiced the Beginner's Exercise, which we'll come to below, when she *wasn't* triggered, she was able to start developing the skill of conditioning her brain and body to produce lower levels of stress chemicals, and higher levels of "feel-good" chemicals, so that she was better prepared for those triggering situations. She did this in the same way that she would have run short distances, increasing them gradually, if training for a marathon. Getting off the couch and running even a mile without conditioning the body to adjust to that level of physical activity is unrealistic. On the other hand, by running up and down the street, and then around the block, and gradually building the stamina and muscles that would support running longer distances, the body is able to build up to that demand.

Think of practicing the Beginner's Exercise every day when you're *not* triggered, just as you would running training or developing the skill of playing a musical instrument. Rather than waiting until the day of a marathon to start running, or the night of a concert to start playing a musical instrument, you would prepare by practicing in the time leading up to the marathon or concert. In the same way, it would be very difficult, if not impossible, to use this exercise in the middle of being emotionally triggered without having built up the skill beforehand through practice.

Apart from being able to change how you're feeling in the moment, conditioning your brain and body to feel good more of the time, and being able to access your cognitive thinking on demand this skill will also help you to change those negative childhood memories (coming up in Chapter 3) that are currently providing the references that "prove" the limiting beliefs that are holding you back.

Since it is the negative emotions (the survival response) that makes it difficult—if not impossible—to change negative memories, bringing down those stress chemicals and replacing them with "feel-good" chemicals is the first step in changing adverse, implicit childhood memories to the opposite, positive, and empowering while keeping the explicit memory of what originally happened.

Take Your Brain for a Test Drive

Think of someone or something you love, such as a person or animal. Nothing with any negative connections, in other words no associations with worry, loss, guilt, or regret—just love. Alice started out by using her younger brother for this exercise, but she couldn't get results. We discovered that it was because her brother had passed away a few years earlier, and she naturally felt pain and loss combined with the love. When she switched to using her beloved cat instead, she was able to achieve the change in her brain chemistry.

If you can't think of a person or animal, you could choose a place or activity you love. Or even an object (like a favorite pair of shoes or a car). Something that, when you think of it, creates a feeling of love or expansion. For example: babies, pets, a favorite animal, gardening, trees, sunsets, and hobbies.

When Odille took a group of businessmen through this exercise a few years ago, one of them used Hawaii as his subject. That was the first time we'd had someone use a place instead of a person or animal, but it worked perfectly for him, and it's worked for many others since. Another client used a stick insect she'd rescued. Choose whatever helps you to feel love when you think of it.

The Beginner's Exercise

Once you have a "subject" go through this little exercise:

1. Take a deep breath, close your eyes, and think of your favorite color again. Imagine being surrounded by that beautiful color and allow yourself to fully focus on how lovely it is.
2. Now, think of that "subject" you love. Imagine holding that person, animal, place, or activity, in your arms, in a hug. (As you imagine this, and really focus on it, your brain will start to produce the "feel-good" chemicals endorphins, serotonin, and oxytocin.)
3. Notice the feeling of love in your chest or solar plexus and imagine it as a ball of light or energy.
4. Imagine that light or energy spreading down to your toes, up to the top of your head, and out to your fingertips so that you're now full of that light or energy. This increases the level of those "feel-good" chemicals still further. Then, imagine that light or energy overflowing from you, and filling the room you're in.

Congratulations! You just changed your brain and body chemistry!

A Note from Odille:

Don't worry if the feeling wasn't very strong—or even if you didn't feel it at all. It can take time and practice to experience the effects, depending on the levels of stress chemicals already in your system.

When I first started practicing this technique, I experienced the good feelings for no more than a few seconds, and even then, it felt uneasy. I'd been living in an intense state of stress for so long that my body was very uncomfortable with the good feelings. It was almost painful. I treated the exercise like physical stretching—practicing gently for just a few seconds at a time and stopping when it became too uncomfortable, then coming back to it later for a little more.

Gradually, I was able to build up to feeling the good feelings for longer and longer periods of time, until it became my default chemical (emotional) state. Of course, I still get triggered occasionally (that's part of being human), but I've gone from being constantly stressed to feeling calm, peaceful, and happy most of the time. I've never been back to that state of despair, anger, pain, and hopelessness I experienced up to the end of 2015—and I've certainly never gone back to the emotional and mental place I was in as I sat in my car, in front of that brick wall in 2008. In fact, Steve finds it difficult to imagine me as a stressed person at all, since we only met in February 2017, after I'd already changed my brain and body chemistry and childhood memories.

Emotional State Conditioning

Think of it like physical fitness. If you haven't worked out before, it may take a little while before you're able to run up and down the street without getting out of breath. But if you ran a little every day, your body would automatically build stamina and become conditioned for fitness.

Eventually, you would be able to run further—you might even sign up for a marathon. It's all about the incremental physiological changes your body automatically makes as it adapts to the new activity, building muscles and stamina.

Emotional State Conditioning is the same. Practicing that little Beginner's Exercise every day, several times a day (as you can see it only takes a few seconds) will build your "emotional stamina" and allow your brain and body to become conditioned to producing those "feel-good" chemicals more frequently. And it will get easier and more noticeable the more you do it.

As Alice practiced the exercise consistently, she started to notice it was becoming easier and easier to recover from being triggered by the lack of response from others. It wasn't a smooth, straight line—just like getting physically fit, there were times when it was more difficult or when she felt like she'd gone back to her old patterns. But as she continued to practice, she developed the skill to the point where she was triggered less frequently, and— importantly—when she *was* triggered, she was able to pull herself out of the negative emotions more quickly.

RECAP:

- Negative thoughts trigger stress chemicals that take the cognitive-thinking part of the brain offline.
- Positive thoughts trigger "feel-good" chemicals that allow blood to return to the cognitive-thinking part of the brain.
- Stress chemicals are stronger than "feel-good" chemicals—we need them for survival—which is why it's easier to feel bad than to feel good.

Although Alice was eventually able to change her emotional state more easily, and felt good more of the time, she kept finding herself in situations where people seemed to ignore or disregard her. She continued to be attracted to men who were emotionally unavailable, and she still found herself unable to rely on her close friends to be there for her when she needed them. Her negative implicit childhood memories of being rejected and ignored were still "proving" her self-image and worldview (*I'm unworthy and unlovable*) and determining her perception, choices, and decisions… ultimately, leading to the same recurring patterns. As we'll explain in the next chapter, once we helped her to change the negative memories, those patterns also changed—automatically.

So, now you know how to drive, let's talk about how you ended up where you are…and how to use this little brain-chemistry exercise to get to where you want to be.

Pillar Two

CHANGING THE GPS— CHILDHOOD MEMORY TRANSFORMATION (CMT)

In 200 Yards, Make a U-Turn

I f you wanted to drive from the city to the beach, and you knew how to drive, but your GPS was still set for the city, every time you started heading toward the beach, your GPS would guide you back to the city. Change those GPS coordinates to match the beach location, and you'll automatically be guided to that destination. The references from childhood experiences that "prove" who we are and how the world works are the GPS coordinates the unconscious part of the brain is currently using. Change those references—the "evidence" that "proves" *I'm not good enough*, for example—and the beliefs, patterns, unconscious behaviors, choices, and experiences change automatically.

> *"Our first experiences create the filters through which all new experiences must pass."*
> —Dr. Bruce Perry[39]

Another way to think of childhood memories is as the roots of plants. Imagine your life is a garden. The things you'd like to change are the weeds. Addressing the events, circumstances, and even beliefs you can see now, as

---

39 Oprah Winfrey & Bruce Perry. (2021). What Happened to You? (Flatiron Books: An Oprah Book, 2021).

an adult, is like cutting off the leaves and branches, and even the stem of a weed. It's okay. And for a while, you won't see the weed. But, naturally, that weed will grow back because the roots are still in place.

In order to end up with the flowers you want instead of the weeds, you have to take out the roots of those weeds and replace them with the seeds of the flowers you want to see in your garden—and then, of course, water those flowers until they are able to survive on their own. In other words, you need to change the negative childhood memories (removing the roots of the weeds) to the opposite, positive, and empowering (planting the seeds of the flowers you want) and play those new memories in your mind until they're established (watering those flowers until they're able to survive on their own).

One of our clients, Debby, had tried everything to change her compulsion to please others. She knew that she was a "people-pleaser," and she recognized the behaviors and choices that led her to feeling resentful and taken advantage of. But no matter how hard she tried to change those choices and behaviors, she kept finding herself in the same situations. She'd try to create boundaries, but over and over, she'd still agree to do things she didn't want to do and would feel a constant underlying anxiety that people would be angry with her. And the worst thing was, no matter how much she tried to please others, her anxiety remained.

In the background, Debby's brain was referring to the implicit memories from her childhood, of parents who were constantly stressed and dealing with financial struggles. Debby had spent her childhood trying to make her parents feel better, trying to make them okay, but of course, making her parents feel better was not within that little girl's power. As an adult, her brain still referred to the "evidence" that proved her self-image and worldview: Who she is—her role—is to try to make others feel better, and they never do. That's what life is. That's "normal." Those were the GPS coordinates her brain was accustomed to referring to and keeping her in alignment with.

Once she changed those childhood memories to the opposite, positive, and empowering—which we'll discuss in Chapter 5—her drive to please others automatically, naturally, and authentically disappeared. Once she replaced those childhood memories with memories of her parents being relaxed, safe, kind, compassionate, happy, fun, and abundant, her "people-pleasing" tendency was automatically replaced with authentic kindness and compassion that came out of a strong, secure, loving self-image and worldview. She no longer needed to set boundaries because when someone asked her to do something she didn't want to do, her brain now referred to those new memories that *proved* she's safe and loved. As a result, her natural, automatic, unconscious response in this situation was to say no, in a kind, compassionate way that set that boundary while still enabling her to feel secure, safe, and confident within herself. Now she doesn't *believe* she's loved, worthy, and safe—she *knows* it.

In Chapter 5, we'll take you through the step-by-step process of exactly how to identify and then change your own negative childhood memories to achieve the changes you want in your life. First, though, it's important that you have a foundation of the concepts.

As Debby tried to stop being a "people-pleaser" by setting more boundaries, changing the way she spoke to people, or even avoiding people altogether. At first, her brain would search for another way to experience the feeling of the need to please. She would often find herself in another situation where she would have those same feelings. Despite her conscious efforts, she would unconsciously find a different relationship or different work situation, to keep repeating that pattern of needing to please. However, once she changed those childhood memories of trying to make her parents happy, she automatically and unconsciously began to make different choices and was naturally and authentically able to maintain healthy personal boundaries.

Whatever a person is dealing with, the answer is always to change the roots—the implicit childhood memories that support that person's experience. For example: If you wanted to change the experience of feeling trapped in a job by leaving the job ("cutting off what you can see of the weed"), you would eventually find yourself back in a similar situation—for example: being in another job you didn't enjoy, feeling trapped in a relationship, or finding yourself in a difficult situation with a neighbor, with financial struggles, or suffering from a physical condition.

In every moment, the brain is processing information from external stimuli and comparing it to the references it has stored from previous experiences in order to know how to react and respond.

Most of us think of childhood as over. Something that happened in the past, something that no longer has a direct impact on our lives. However, consider the following:

You see a mirror. How do you know that what you're looking at is "a mirror"?
How do you know that what you're seeing in it is your reflection?
How do you know it's not dangerous?
How do you feel when you see a mirror? Do you like mirrors? Do you feel resistance to looking in mirrors or have some other emotion?
Can you recall when you learned about mirrors?
Can you recall how you learned that you like or dislike looking in the mirror?

Unless something significant happened that created a link in your brain between mirrors and an emotional event, you probably can't remember when you originally learned what a mirror is and how to respond to it. It's automatic. And it's what's known in psychology as "implicit memory."

Implicit memory is how we respond, automatically, to experiences. It's why we don't have to consciously think everything through before choosing a reaction. It's also why someone can "push our buttons." It's why we feel triggered.

Remember Alice's recurring pattern of being attracted to emotionally unavailable men? As we taught her the techniques for finding and changing negative childhood memories, Alice discovered a link between her choices in relationships as an adult and her experiences of being neglected by both parents as a child. Her parents were constantly stressed, ambitious in their careers, and had a busy social life. They hadn't planned to have children. Alice was an accident and was treated that way throughout her childhood. She wasn't physically abused or neglected, and there was nothing she could pinpoint in her parents' behavior that was actively negative. They just didn't show her affection. They made sure she was fed, clothed, and educated. But, being fully focused on their own careers and social lives, they paid no more attention to her than was necessary to keep her physically safe.

The result was that the unconscious part of Alice's brain created implicit memories from those experiences that in turn provided the structure of her self-image and worldview of *I'm not important* and *I'm unlovable*. Memories of desperately wanting her parents' love, attention, affection, and approval but being sidelined and dismissed, were stored in her brain as proof that she was unlovable, and that other people and material things were always more important than her. Childhood experiences of watching her parents laughing and connecting with others but seeming to look right through her reinforced that self-image and worldview as she grew up.

In her interactions with other children and adults, everything Alice experienced was automatically filtered through that self-image and worldview. And of course, she responded according to those filtered experiences, not according to objective reality.

When a child in her class invited her to sit with a group of friends during lunch, the unconscious part of Alice's brain referred to the "evidence" from earlier childhood experiences that "proved" she was unworthy and unlovable, and it automatically triggered stress chemicals that caused feelings of anxiousness, self-doubt, and mistrust. So, she declined the invitation, and chose to sit alone, which felt "safer."

That choice was seen by the group of girls as a rejection and "weird" and it wasn't long before Alice—unintentionally and unconsciously—stepped into the role of outsider and loner. She no longer received invitations for lunchtime company. Neither was she invited to birthday parties, and she was the last to be picked for any team activities. Not only was every experience filtered through her existing self-image and worldview of *I'm not important* and *I'm unworthy*, but every such experience also added further evidence that continued to *prove* that self-image and worldview. Her life became a constant cycle of unconscious choices based on previous experience, and new experiences *proving* that those choices were justified.

The momentum of that cycle had created who Alice was as an adult and her reality. In every moment, the unconscious part of her brain was referring to the "fact" that she was unimportant and unloved, and that no one cared about her. This played out in two main ways:

1. Whenever she met someone, the unconscious part of her brain that scans micro expressions, gestures, and tone of voice—comparing them to implicit memories to determine how to respond—would discount anything that didn't fit into her self-image and worldview. Anyone who was attentive was unattractive to her. Equally, anyone who showed unconscious signs of fitting into the pattern of being emotionally unavailable was considered perfect.

2. When someone didn't reply to her because they were distracted or busy, or even if they were unable to respond because they didn't receive the message, Alice's brain would refer to the "fact" that she was unimportant and unlovable, which would then automatically trigger the stress chemicals that created feelings of emotional pain and hurt. Those feelings triggered matching thoughts, and the neural connections of those thoughts triggered yet more of those stress chemicals.

It Makes No Logical Sense

Remember that the unconscious part of the brain has no ability to use logic or reason. No matter how much you may hate being in the city and *want* to be at the beach, if the coordinates in your GPS are set for the city, the GPS cannot reason that it needs to guide you to the beach instead. It will simply guide you according to the coordinates that are currently set. In the same way, no matter how much you don't want to experience pain, rejection, financial struggle, or despair, if those are the only references the unconscious part of your brain has to draw on, it will automatically keep bringing you back to that state.

RECAP:

- Implicit (unconscious) childhood memories determine our self-image and worldview.
- The unconscious part of the brain can't tell the difference between reality and imagination, can't use logic or reason in the way that the conscious mind does, and can't judge something as unrealistic

Childhood memories are the GPS coordinates that determine your destination—automatically. Whatever you're experiencing in your life now is because of the references, from childhood experiences, that the unconscious part of your brain refers to[40]. Change those childhood memories, and you change your experiences, automatically.

But…can memories really be changed?

---

40   Bruce Ecker. "Memory Reconsolidation Understood and Misunderstood." International Journal of Neuropsychotherapy. 3(1), 2015: 2–46. doi: 10.12744/ijnpt.2015.0002-0046.
　　"Clinicians, however, regularly observe phenomenology showing that an extremely wide range of other conditions also are rooted in and driven by implicit memory (Ecker et al., 2012; Ecker & Toomey, 2008; Toomey & Ecker, 2007; Schore, 2003; Siegel, 2006)."

Can Memories Really be Changed?

According to the latest in neuroscience, memories are neither accurate nor permanent[41]. In fact, memories are automatically updated according to new experiences.

> *"Even the precious memories of our childhood can actually be shaped and reshaped like a ball of clay... Memory errors can be considered the norm, not the exception."*
> —Dr. Julia Shaw[42]

If you've ever had a conversation with family or friends about an event you all experienced, you may have found that everyone seems to remember it differently.

One of our clients shared the following:

"He told me that he was bitten on his lip by a dog when he was about

---

41   Donna J. Bridge & Ken A. Paller "Neural Correlates of Reactivation and Retrieval-Induced Distortion." Journal of Neuroscience. 32(35), 2012:12144–151. DOI: https://doi.org/10.1523/JNEUROSCI.1378-12.2012.
      https://www.jneurosci.org/content/32/35/12144.
42   Julia Shaw. (2016). The Memory Illusion: Remembering, Forgetting, and the Science of False Memory. (Canada: Doubleday).

three, but it wasn't him, it was his brother who was bitten on the lip and still has the scar."

If memories are already inaccurate and changing, and we have the ability to change them intentionally, why not change them to benefit and empower ourselves? Memory Reconsolidation Therapy is already being used to treat those suffering from PTSD[43]. However, one of the reasons the results are inconsistent may be that Memory Reconsolidation is usually used for the memories of the events that appear to have caused the PTSD in the adult, instead of the original childhood memories that provided the references for those events.

Not everyone who experiences the same traumatic event develops PTSD. In fact, not everyone who experiences the same event experiences it in the same way at all. As the event is happening, each person's brain refers to their own references from previous experiences to determine what this new experience means and how to respond to it.

Everything we experience is filtered through the structure of who we are and how the world works[44]—based on childhood experiences—and then that new information is added to the existing structure.

For example: Two babies are born at the same time, in the same town.

Mary is born to parents who are loving, financially secure, happy, and fulfilled, who have effective emotional coping skills, and who can't wait to meet their new baby girl.

Jane is born to parents who are stressed, struggling financially, aren't ready for a child, and whose emotional coping skills involve shouting, and "the silent treatment."

43   Emiliano Merlo, Amy L. Milton, & Barry J. Everitt. "Enhancing Cognition by Affecting Memory Reconsolidation." Current Opinion in Behavioral Sciences. 4, 2015: 41–47. https://doi.org/10.1016/j.cobeha.2015.02.003.

44   RIKEN. "Fishing For Memories: How Long-Term Memories are Processed to Guide Behavior." ScienceDaily. May 2013. www.sciencedaily.com/releases/2013/05/130516123914.htm.

Every individual's life experience is, of course, unique—which means that the structure of who a person is and how the world works for them is unique. As these babies grow, each girl's brain will be interpreting all their experiences automatically and forming a structure of meaning.

Mary's brain will interpret the complex combination of loving and caring experiences from her early childhood, from both of her parents, to create a structure that includes:

I'm loved, valuable, and heard; I light up a room; life is abundant; I'm clever; everyone loves me; and *life is fun.* All those references boil down to one thing: *I'm safe.*

As humans, we're not equipped to survive alone. From birth, we're completely helpless and dependent on those around us. Therefore, part of our automatic survival instinct is to please those around us so that they will prioritize feeding and protecting us. If we are loved, valuable, and the center of their attention, we're safe—we will be fed and protected above anyone else, which, to the unconscious part of the brain, means survival.

Note from Odille

Survival and protection are not just about food, clothing, and shelter. I remember, as a child, hearing adults say: "Oh, she's just looking for attention!" Saying, "That child is just looking for attention," is like saying, "That child just wants oxygen." Instinctively, attention is survival. "If I am rejected from my tribe, I'll die." Children don't just want attention, they need it. It's part of the unconscious survival instinct.

Surviving School

Now, let's look at Jane. Jane's brain interprets the arguments between her parents, impatience, tension, and lack of affection, compassion, and kindness to mean: *I'm not important; it's not safe to have fun; I'm not valu-able or heard; I don't matter; I'm not understood; there's not enough;* and *stress is normal.* All those references boil down to: *I'm not safe.*

Out of these references, both girls will develop a unique set of survival skills and coping mechanisms as they go through life.

Fast forward now, and both girls are starting at the same school.

Each girl arrives in this new environment full of new experiences and people with a completely different set of references that "prove" who they are, how the world works, and how to survive.

Mary, with her structure of *I'm safe and life is fun* will automatically express confidence because her brain contains "proof" that she's safe and that people love her.

Jane, with her structure of *I'm not safe and life is stressful* will automat-ically express symptoms that reflect this. Depending on the combination of references, she may appear disinterested, anxious, or irritable, or she may even come across as over-confident and bossy. The first impression she makes will depend on the unique combination of coping skills that have developed automatically and unconsciously through her experiences so far.

Since Mary's brain and body are conditioned to produce mostly "feel-good" chemicals and she has normal levels of stress, her prefrontal cortex will be "online" most of the time. This will mean she's able to concen-trate, process information, problem-solve, and retain and recall informa-tion more easily and effectively. That, of course, leads to her doing well in school, academically. She's also, because of her references, a natural "team player," so she fits in well with groups, sports, and activities.

On the other hand, since Jane's brain and body are conditioned to produce mostly stress chemicals, and she lives in a state of "fight-or-flight," her prefrontal cortex is "offline" most of the time. She doesn't have access to that cognitive-thinking part of her brain. So, no matter how much she may want to do well in school, she literally cannot access the part of her brain needed for problem-solving, communication, concentration, absorbing, comprehending, processing, and recalling information. She also hasn't developed the social skills needed to fit in—and, most importantly, because her references "prove" that she's not safe, her coping skills have automatically developed to make her either a people-pleaser or wary of others.

You can see how each of these girls will develop very differently throughout their school experience.

Now, imagine both girls have the same experience of a bully saying something mean to them.

In that moment, Mary's previous references "prove" she's not in danger. Mary may find the bully's remark mildly annoying; she may not think it worth paying attention to, she may find it funny, or she may not even register it at all.

In that moment, Jane's previous references "prove" she's in danger. Jane's brain pumps more stress chemicals into her system, and her experience of the bully's remark will be one that further proves she's unworthy, stupid, or whatever that experience means to her through the filters of the structure that already exists in her brain.

The bully's words, expression, tone of voice, and body language will mean something different to each girl, based on what references they already have.

And, of course, the encounter with the bully is not just about that experience. Jane's reaction to it will have a knock-on effect on her experiences with everything and everyone, moving forward. Mary's reaction to that experience (or the lack of it) will have little to no effect on her interactions, moving forward.

According to the CDC, Adverse Childhood Experiences (ACEs) can negatively impact education, job opportunities, and earning potential[45].

As adults, Mary and Jane are working in the same office, and earn the same salary. However, while Mary is able not only to save, but also able to invest and build a solid financial foundation, Jane is in debt and struggles to pay her bills. In addition to everything else that's in place already in the brains of both women, every decision (including financial judgment, ability to assess risk, and awareness of opportunities) is determined by the "evidence" in those original childhood memories, that "proves" who they are and how the world works.

For example, Mary feels confident asking for a raise because she *knows*—from the evidence in her implicit childhood memories—that she's worth it. She also has the ability to communicate her worth and ask for that raise in a strategic manner. On the other hand, Jane *knows*— from the evidence in *her* implicit childhood memories—that she's unworthy. And that affects the way in which she asks for a raise, if she ever even asks at all.

When an opportunity comes up that would result in financial loss, Mary's brain filters that information through the structure of *I'm worthy and the world is an abundant and safe place,* and since she has access to her cognitive thinking, she recognizes the risks, so she turns it down. Jane's brain filters the same opportunity through different references that "prove" that she's unworthy, is undeserving, and that stress is normal, and it seems like a good idea. Since she has "proof" from the implicit memories from her childhood, that there's "not enough," she also has a fear of missing out. This fear causes her brain to overlook the risks, and she invests in the opportunity. She ends up losing money.

---

45   "Preventing Adverse Childhood Experiences." Center for Disease Control and Prevention. April 6, 2021. https://www.cdc.gov/violenceprevention/aces/fastfact.html.

Another opportunity comes up that would be financially beneficial. Mary's brain filters the opportunity through the "fact" that she is worthy, and since she has access to her prefrontal cortex, she's able to process the information and make a decision based on strategy and problem-solving, which leads to an increase in her financial situation. Jane's brain filters the same opportunity through the "facts" of, *I'm not safe* and *stress is normal.* And, since the improved financial situation would not be in alignment with that self-image and worldview, her brain discounts it and labels it as a bad option. Stress chemicals are pumped into her system, she doesn't have access to her cognitive thinking, and she finds reasons to turn down that opportunity, or procrastinate until it's too late.

Now, let's say Jane finds a way to change the implicit memories from her childhood that "prove" she's unworthy, not safe, and that stress is normal, to the opposite, positive, and empowering. In other words, she replaces her original childhood memories with *new* childhood memories that are similar to Mary's experiences.

Is it Wrong to Change Memories?

While Jane will still have *declarative* memories of what originally happened—consciously she knows what she experienced in her childhood—her new *implicit* memories (unconscious memory) will now automatically provide "proof" that she's worthy, safe, valued, and lights up a room, and that it's safe to have fun and feel good. It's a bit like when you learn a new phone number: When you think of your phone number the new one is the first to come to mind (implicit memory) while you can still consciously and intentionally recall the old one (explicit memory).

The brain is constantly changing and adapting as we experience and learn new information. The ability of the brain to update information based on new experiences is known as neuroplasticity[46]. Experiences are not just physical events. Experiences include imagination (since the unconscious

---

46   Eberhard Fuchs & Gabriele Flügge. "Adult Neuroplasticity: More Than 40 Years of Research." Neural Plasticity. 2014, Article ID541870, 10 pages. https://doi.org/10.1155/2014/541870.

part of the brain can't tell the difference between reality and imagination). As you imagine the new memory, your brain "experiences" it. As you repeat it (firing the same neural patterns), those connections become stronger, and the memory becomes established as fact. Adding strong emotions to the new memory causes the brain to prioritize consolidating the memory for long-term storage[47].

Now when opportunities come up, with these new implicit memories not only will Jane have new references that affect her perception, judgment, and risk-assessment, she'll also (due to the lack of stress chemicals in her system) have access to her prefrontal cortex—her cognitive thinking. Consequently, she will automatically make decisions and take actions that are in alignment with that new self-image and worldview.

When we helped Alice to change her childhood memories of her relationship with her parents to the opposite, positive and empowering, her self-image and worldview changed accordingly. As a result, her perception, choices, decisions, and judgment also changed. She found she was no longer triggered when someone didn't respond to her, and—most impressively—she found she was no longer attracted to emotionally unavailable men. In fact, she started finding kind and compassionate men attractive.

Alice can still remember, consciously, what her parents were really like when she was a child, but her implicit childhood memories are now those of love, affection, connection, and validation from both parents. The result is that although she can still recall what originally happened, the unconscious part of her brain now refers to new evidence that "proves" she's loved, valuable, important, and safe. And that completely changed her self-image and worldview (and in turn, her life experiences) to the opposite, positive, and empowering.

---

47   James L. McGaugh. "Making Lasting Memories: Remembering the Significant." PNAS. 110 (Supplement 2), 2013: 10402–07. https://www.pnas.org/content/110/Supplement_2/10402.

Note from Odille:

When I think of my childhood now, it's filled with memories of love, affection, kindness, compassion, safety, fun, freedom, peace, and abundance, but I can still tell you what really happened.

I can still tell you that from the age of six in Durban, South Africa, I worked before school at 5.30 a.m., after school, weekends, and holidays (including Christmas Day). I worked in heavy costumes and in humid heat. Always on duty, wishing I was playing on the beach with the other children across the road. I can still tell you that there was no payment for that work, so, in addition to an over-the-top work ethic, I developed the belief that I don't deserve to be paid. I can still tell you of being beaten, the fear, the shame, the bullying at school, growing up without a father, financial struggle, emotional pain, and of other damaging experiences. I can tell you about all of that because, while those memories no longer form the foundation of who I am and my worldview, they are still declarative memories. They are still there if I need or choose to access them. But it is the new childhood I created in the unconscious part of my brain that provides the "evidence" for who I am and what I experience in my life now. I have happy memories from my childhood as well, and I've kept those of course. We can keep the positive memories, and just change the negative ones.

My parents and grandparents did the very best they could, considering their own childhood references. My mother and her parents each started working at four years old. They had unimaginably tough lives, with suffering and struggle at the core, which formed their reality of who they were and how the world worked for them. From the self-image and worldview created by those childhood experiences, they were amazing. From the self-image and worldview created by their childhood references, through their eyes, they gave us the most wonderful childhood—a childhood they could only have dreamed of.

It's Over, But it's Not Over

When Elaine came to one of our workshops, she had already been through two years of conventional talk therapy. She knew that her traumatic childhood had created the depression, anxiety, and panic attacks she'd experienced for so many years, but spending time recalling and exploring those childhood memories had done nothing to reduce the emotional pain she continued to suffer. She'd been told to let go of the childhood loss and abuse since it was no longer happening. While she could consciously reason that her childhood was over, the unconscious part of her brain continued to keep her in a state of hypervigilance and stress as if it were all still going on.

Reliving negative experiences causes the brain to retrigger that fight-or-flight state of survival over and over. Since the unconscious part of the brain can't tell the difference between reality and imagination, can't use logic or reason, has no sense of time, and can't judge something as unrealistic, it produces the same state when you think about the memories as it would if the events were happening now.

Reliving negative memories is not the solution. Reliving negative memories keeps you stuck in a time warp of suffering.

RECAP:

- Memories are neither accurate nor permanent and are already changing and being updated.
- Memory reconsolidation ("memory editing") is already being used to treat PTSD.
- Changing a memory means imagining the event differently, and then repeating that new version until it's established (as you would learn a new phone number).
- Just as when you change the coordinates in your GPS, you, as the driver, can still remember your previous destinations—while the unconscious part of your brain will refer to the new empowering memories, you will still be able to remember what originally happened (explicit memories).

Chapter 5

How to Change Your Brain's GPS Coordinates

C hanging memories is as simple as imagining them differently.

Think of your front door. And, whatever color it is, make it white, in your mind. Now, imagine it's blue. If you can't suddenly imagine it as blue, imagine taking out a pot of blue paint and paint it blue in your mind. Now, make it red. Now, make it yellow. Put some purple flowers on it.

You can probably imagine your door as a different color fairly easily because, presumably, you have no emotional attachment to your front door. And if you were to continue imagining your front door as blue, over and over, your brain would connect your front door with that color. Then, every time you think of your door, that's the color that would automatically come to mind. Of course, you would also always be able to remember, consciously, that your front door is white (declarative memory).

So, can memories be changed as easily as you changed the color of your front door?

The difference between changing the color of your door in your mind and changing a negative memory is the emotions behind it. As we recall a negative memory, the brain automatically prompts the production of stress chemicals to go with it. And, as we know, stress chemicals are part of the survival state and are therefore designed to attract, and hold, our attention on the "danger." Trying to imagine that instead of being beaten, we were actually having fun and playing table tennis isn't going to work while we still feel the associated fear, anger, humiliation, and other negative emotions (the stress chemicals are still in our system).

But if we lower the level of stress chemicals first, so that we no longer feel any negative emotion when recalling that memory, we can then imagine the memory differently—just like the color of the front door. Think of a guard dog that has been trained to bark and attack whenever anyone comes to the door. Trying to change a memory of being beaten to a happy memory of playing table tennis is like trying to reason with that guard dog, and telling the dog it's okay, that it's just a friend at the door. The dog is in protection mode, so telling him there's no danger is not enough to quieten him.

> *"The greatest mind control is control over your own mind."*
> —Tom Bilyeu, The Impact Theory[48]

It's important to remember that whatever happened back then is no longer happening now. We're not going to forget what happened, we're just going to move it from implicit or nondeclarative memory (proving who we are and how the world works) to explicit or declarative memory (something that happened).

The goal is to change our implicit memories to "prove" the results that we *want* to experience in our lives, moving forward.

Since that unconscious part of the brain can't tell the difference between reality and imagination, can't use logic or reason, and can't judge something as unrealistic, it will believe whatever we give it. It will believe

48   Tom Bilyeu. "Impact Theory." Impact Theory. https://impacttheory.com/ accessed October 10, 2021.

the new memories while we are still consciously able to recall what originally happened.

> **NOTE:** *As stated earlier, do not attempt to address trauma on your own. If you have trauma memories, be sure to get help from a professional therapist or certified Remmert Method Practitioner. The following guidance is for non-trauma memories and issues.*

The Detective Work

Although the end result we're aiming for is to have had a whole new childhood, you can also use these steps to address an isolated issue. The following questions will help you to identify specific childhood memories that support a current issue.

It's important to remember that any current issues you are experiencing, and the corresponding childhood memories that cause them, may be different topics. Bear in mind that the unconscious part of your brain that creates, maintains, and refers to these memories doesn't have the ability to use logic or reason the way the conscious mind does. Let's say you're dealing with a lack of self-confidence.

1. Ask yourself: *"How do I know (or what's the worst thing about it)?"* For example: *"How do I know I don't have self-confidence?"* Or *"What's the worst thing about not having self-confidence?"*

2. Ask yourself: *"How does that feel?"* For example: *"I feel hopeless,"* or *"I feel scared,"* or *"I feel like I'm held back from doing what I want to do,"* or *"I feel pressure."*

3. Ask yourself: *"Where in my childhood did I feel that same feeling?"* (NOTE: It may not be the same topic, but will be the same feeling.) For example: Hearing parents arguing; being unable to express yourself; being bullied in school; being blamed for something

you didn't do; being physically held back; unattainable expectations. It may not make logical sense, but whatever comes to you from childhood, if it's negative, it needs to be changed anyway.

Make a list of the negative memories that come to you—just one or two words that identify those memories for you and the approximate age you were when it happened, no details or description needed. For example:

Kitchen, shoes, eight years old.

The age doesn't need to be accurate, just guess approximately how old you were.

Organize the memories in order of age, from youngest to oldest. Think back to the image of a weed. There are lots of small roots attached to the larger ones. But you don't have to remove every one of those small roots. You can pull up the main roots, and as you do so, the smaller ones will come up at the same time. Then you can remove just those smaller ones that remain behind. Therefore, as you change your key early memories, others will automatically be changed as well. You can then just change those that remain.

Unexpected Childhood Links

At one of our weekend workshops in Seattle, WA, we were checking in with the participants, when Michele asked for help finding the childhood memories that were creating her challenges with money. Here's how the process went for her:

Issue: Michele was in a full-time job doing work that she wasn't passionate about. She desperately wanted to be able to do what she loved for a living instead. She had been trying, for a couple of years, to get into a financial position where she would be able to leave her job and start her own consulting business. But each time she tried to save up, or increase her income, something would always happen to make sure she stayed financially reliant on her job. We advised Michele to ask herself the Detective Questions:

1. How do I know it's a problem?
   A: *Because I'm not financially able to leave my full-time job.*

2. How does that feel?
   A: *It feels like I'm being held back from doing what I really want to do.*

3. Where in my childhood did I feel that same feeling? Remember, it may have nothing to do with money or business, but it will be the same feeling.
   A: *My parents wouldn't let me change schools.*

   Michele remembered that she desperately wanted to attend a particular high school, but her parents refused to allow her to change schools. She recognized that, although that experience had nothing to do with money or business, the feeling of being held back and prevented from doing what she wanted to do was the same.

Now that Michele was an adult, and her parents were no longer holding her back from doing what she wanted to do, money was playing the role of her parents. While Michele was consciously doing her best to get into a financial situation that would allow her to leave her full-time job and start her own business, the unconscious part of her brain was referring to the "fact" that it was "normal" to be held back from doing what she wanted to do.

Just as Alice's brain filtered her experiences through the self-image and worldview of *I'm not important* and *I'm unlovable*, which affected her perception, choices, decisions, and the way she experienced other people, Michele's brain was filtering her experiences through the self-image and worldview of: *I'm held back from doing what I desperately want to do*. The unconscious part of her brain referred to the experience of being held back from attending the high school she wanted to attend, along with other memories that felt similar (those GPS coordinates), which affected her ability to notice professional opportunities, her choices and decisions regarding finances, and her ability to assess risk—she was still aligned with being held back from doing what she wanted to do (the "destination" that matched those GPS coordinates).

What if You Can't Remember Childhood Memories?

If you can't find any childhood memories, just start creating new memories from scratch, using the Bookmark Memories in Chapter 12 of this book. And as you start to do that, you may find that negative memories pop up—and you can then change those.

Changing a Negative Memory—Step-by-Step

Changing a memory is as simple as imagining it differently. Since the unconscious part of your brain can't tell the difference between reality and imagination, can't use logic or reason, and can't judge something as unrealistic, it will believe whatever you give it. Just as when you watch a movie, your brain and body automatically respond as if the movie is real. You feel the feelings of fear, anticipation, joy, relief, and love, even though what you're watching is not real. It's just images on a screen. In the same way, your brain and body will respond to whatever you're imagining.

Since it is the negative emotions that keep us from being able to change negative memories to the opposite, positive, and empowering, we need to address those first. Once we've brought down those negative emotions (stress chemicals), we can then change the memory by imagining it differently, and then establish it through repetition—just as you would learn a new phone number—and by adding positive emotions.

Bringing Down the Negative Emotions

You've already learned in Chapter 2 how to change your brain chemistry, and we're going to use that technique again here to change a negative memory.

1. Take a deep breath, close your eyes, and think of your favorite color. Imagine being surrounded by that color and allow yourself

to feel the feeling of that beautiful color.

2. Now, think of your subject—that person, animal, place, or activity you love (with no negative emotions attached—no guilt, longing, or regret etc.)—and imagine holding that subject, in your arms, in a hug.

3. Focus in on the feeling—the physical feeling of that love—in your chest or solar plexus. If you have trouble feeling it at first, think about all the reasons you love this person, animal, place, or activity.

4. Imagine that feeling of love as a ball of light or energy, and imagine it spreading down to your toes, up to the top of your head, and out to your fingertips, so that you're now full of that light, that love for your subject.

5. Now, imagine "pressing pause" on that for a moment, and go to the first (earliest) memory on your list. (NOTE: Remember not to address trauma memories on your own—seek help from a professional.) Briefly notice how strong any negative emotions are in this memory from zero to 10. Don't take longer than a few seconds to notice this.

   Think of these negative emotions as a hot bath. You want to just very briefly dip your toe into the water to see how hot it is, rather than getting into it.

6. Next, "press pause" on that, and go back to imagining being surrounded by your favorite color. Allow yourself to fully embrace the lovely feeling of that color, and then imagine hugging your subject. Again, to make those good feelings stronger, think of the reasons you love this subject. If it's a person or animal, have they ever done anything funny? Focus in on all those good feelings and imagine that love as a light spreading all the way through your body.

7. Now, "press pause" on that again, and go back to the negative memory. Notice how strong the negative feelings are now. Are they still the same? Are they stronger? Are they weaker? Just spend a few seconds on this—remember, you're just dipping your toe in,

don't fully get into it. If the negative emotions were a seven before, where are they now?

8. Immediately "press pause" on that negative memory and go back once again to imagining being surrounded by your favorite color and hugging your subject. Allow yourself to fully focus on the details of what you love about that color and your subject.

Repeat this process, back and forth (spending much more time in the good feelings than in the negative memory) until there are no negative emotions left in that old memory when you think of it. Then you're ready to move to the next step.

How This Part of the Process Works

When you think of being surrounded by your favorite color and hugging someone or something you love, those neural connections trigger "feel-good" chemicals like endorphins, serotonin, and oxytocin. When you think about that old negative memory, your brain fires different neural connections, and triggers stress chemicals. This is why we want to make sure you don't focus on that memory, and instead, spend only a few seconds noticing it before returning to the good feelings. When you return to your favorite color and the subject you love, your brain stops producing those stress chemicals, and returns to producing the "feel-good" chemicals.

As you do this, back and forth, replacing stress chemicals with "feel-good" chemicals, you'll notice that the negative feelings will decrease, and you will be able to think of the negative memory *without* the negative emotions. That's when you'll be able to "rewire" the rest of the memory by imagining it differently—in the same way you imagined your door being a different color.

If you find the negative emotions are not coming down, check REST AND REPAIR STOPS later in this book, for techniques to help you move forward with this process.

Changing the Memory

Now that you've brought down the negative emotions and you're able to think of that memory without stress chemicals in your system, you can change it by imagining it differently.

Remember, you're not changing your declarative memory of this event—you'll still know what originally happened—you are changing the implicit memory, so your brain will no longer be referring to what happened as "proof" of who you are and how the world works.

Of course, just like changing your GPS, you have complete control over what you change—and what you change it to. This is all about empowering yourself to choose, instead of being at the mercy of "default settings."

Now, as you think about that time in your life, ask yourself what would have been the ideal. What would have been the very best experience? Remind yourself that the unconscious part of your brain cannot use logic or reason, can't tell the difference between reality and imagination, and can't judge something as unrealistic. It will believe whatever you give it. There's also no limit to the budget or to the special effects inside your mind! So you might as well make it the very best it can be.

Ask yourself these questions:

1. What would that little me have preferred to have happened back then?
2. What do I need in my life now?

For example: If you experienced being bullied in school at eight years old, and you are currently worried about your finances, the answers to these questions may be:

1. I was popular in school—everyone loved me, and all the kids admired me.
2. I always had more than enough love, attention, and support from both of my parents. I was safe, loved, and life was full of fun.

You'll notice we didn't answer that second question with *I had lots of money*, and that's because, although it's absolutely fine to include that you had lots of money, money is only a symptom, not a cause. So, by all means include that your family was wealthy, and that you always had plenty of money and the best of everything, but make sure you *also* include an abundance of love, attention, admiration, and security. That is the "currency" that creates your experiences now, as an adult.

Once Michele had changed the memories of her parents holding her back from going to the school she wanted to attend, along with other childhood memories of being held back from doing what she wanted to do, she started to see different options, opportunities, and solutions. She noticed that she was making different choices and was willing to take different action to what she'd been prepared to do before.

Michele now runs her own successful consulting business. She's making her living doing what she loves and helping others. It wasn't about the money. It was about the childhood experiences of being held back.

Example from Steve:

I had an experience with a significant memory that serves as an example of changing a formative childhood reference. It was May 29th, 1971. My family had gathered for Memorial Day weekend and to celebrate my brother's birthday. It was a beautiful spring afternoon. My three brothers and I were playing in the backyard with my grandfather, who was celebrating being three days from retirement, while the rest of the family was engaged in various stages of meal prep.

I didn't see him fall, but what I remember is seeing my grandfather lying face down in the grass. Suddenly the mood of the day shifted to confusion and chaos. Adults were running, crying, frozen. I am not sure who ushered us to the living room of the house, but what I most clearly remember of the rest of that day was sitting on the couch in the living room with my three younger brothers while the events of my grandfather's massive fatal heart attack played out around us: The doctor and ambulance coming and going; my grandmother and uncle sobbing in the kitchen; the confusion and not knowing what was happening. I somehow knew that being the oldest of the children I was responsible for my three younger brothers, but the feeling that I most clearly remember was being "frozen" at the end of the couch. I very vividly remember the stiff texture of that green 1950s couch, and even though the seven-year-old me would not have used this word, the feeling of being "paralyzed" with fear.

As a result of that day, it is clear to see how being "frozen" or "paralyzed" in an extremely anxiety-inducing situation became a coping skill. Whether literally or metaphorically, I would end up "at the end of the couch" feeling shut down and unable to see a way of moving forward through some of the darkest chapters of my life.

When I began the process of transforming this memory, I discovered that the feeling and pattern of being frozen and not knowing what to do had an even earlier reference. As I attempted to reimagine the memory of my grandfather's sudden death at our family gathering, I found that I could not get the memory to change—the feeling of paralysis, not knowing what to do, and the fear were still strong. I had some ideas of how I wanted to reimagine the memory, but it didn't feel "real" and there was much resistance in trying to change it.

Exploring the resistance further, I discovered an earlier memory that I had forgotten about. It did not hold the same emotional charge—in fact, I didn't have any feelings about it at all. I am approximately four or five years old in the scene. I am watching the family doctor (who still did house calls in the 1960s) coming into the house and going to be with my mother, who was in the bathroom. I can see my father's worried face, I can hear my mother crying in the bathroom and I am aware of being alone and frozen in the corner of the kitchen, uncertain of what was going on. I don't ever remember anyone in my family speaking about this incident, and from my adult perspective, I suspect my mother was experiencing severe postpartum depression and the stress of taking care of four children all under the age of five years old. I can also surmise that the little four-year-old me felt confused and frightened, and that his very young parents were also not equipped with the skills of being able to recognize how the situation was impacting their small children.

I was grateful that this earlier memory had emerged as I could see that it was directly related to how the little me responded to the traumatic sudden death of my grandfather. Because this earlier memory did not have any emotional feelings attached to it, I began the process of changing the details of the event. I implemented the use of "Stepping Stone Memories" (described in detail in Chapter 19) to change the data of the story. I surmised that the little me felt helpless and alone and uncertain of what to do in the original memory. I, therefore, created new data where my father is helping me understand what's going on and giving me the responsibility of ushering the doctor to where my mother is. I can hear him encouraging and reassuring me. He also gently instructs me to be with my younger brothers and play with them to help them feel better.

I liked the feeling of empowerment and encouragement this new data provided. I can see my mother emerging from the bathroom with the doctor, who is praising and thanking me for my help. I see my mother smiling. Then, after rehearsing this new data (the Stepping-Stone Memory), I was able to reimagine the scene entirely. Now I see my father and I planning a surprise for my mother. My mother was always a big fan of early rock and roll music, so now in the scene of the new memory, my father is distracting her in another room of the house and gives me the job of escorting a young Elvis Presley and his guitar back to the room where my mother is so that he can serenade her with Love Me Tender.

Now when I think about this new memory, I have a feeling of em-powerment and connection, and a sense of knowing what's happening. The memory feels fun—and I can also hear Elvis singing and my mother singing along with him. As she looks at me, I hear, "...for my darling, I love you, and I always will."

Equipped with this revised earlier memory, I returned to the memory of my grandfather's passing with a completely new experience for the little me. The feeling of being frozen and paralyzed was gone. I engaged in changing data about the old memory (Stepping-Stones) and could easily see my father calmly taking charge and giving me the responsibility of calling the doctor. The doctor arrives quickly and revives my grandfather, and I can see my grandfather hugging my father and me with gratitude for our quick thinking and decisive actions.

After changing the data and meaning of the original memory, I was able to change the entire memory to having my grandfather's WWII pal Marion Morrison (a.k.a. John Wayne) show up as a special guest to the party. I can now see us all listening to my grandfather and his old army buddy John Wayne sharing stories as I sit on the end of the old green couch.

Establishing the New Memory

Memories are established through repetition. You'll have noticed that the key to remembering something is usually to keep remembering it! Each time you recall the event or information, you are firing a particular neural pattern in your brain. You may have heard the phrase, "Cells that fire together wire together"[49]. The phrase was introduced by psychologist Donald Hebb and refers to the theory that when one neuron stimulates another,

---

49   Institute of Science and Technology Austria. "Neuroscientists Discover New Learning Rule for Pattern Completion." ScienceDaily. www.sciencedaily.com/releases/2016/05/160513111839.htm.

repeatedly, the connection between those neurons becomes stronger. It's called Hebb's Rule or Hebbian Theory[50].

This is how, as you repeat the multiplication table, it becomes easier and easier to remember—each time you recite it, the connections between those particular neurons become stronger and more established. So, if you want to learn anything—from historical facts to physical skills—the key is repetition until it becomes automatic.

If that's the case, how is it that you can have experienced an event just once, and be able to recall it without any repetition at all?

This is where emotions come in. When the experience is accompanied by an intense chemical reaction (emotional response) the brain prioritizes it as important[51]. For example, if you were walking past a particular tree and you encountered a bear, your brain would trigger the emergency fight-flight-freeze response, and because of the intensity of the experience, it would also prioritize that memory so that you remember to keep away from that tree in future—for survival.

It's important to remember that when you think about something someone did or said that hurt you, when you think about something you're worried about, when you feel shame, guilt, or any other negative emotional state, your brain produces the same stress chemicals (including adrenaline and cortisol) that it would if you were in physical danger. You'll have noticed that you don't need to be in physical danger to feel fear. You just need to think of something you're worried about—perhaps what others will think of you, for example. Although what someone thinks of you and an actual bear are two completely different experiences, your brain and body will still produce the same stress chemicals in response. And those chemicals will have the same effect on your brain and body.

50   Christian Keysers & Valeria Gazzola. "Hebbian Learning and Predictive Mirror Neurons for Actions, Sensations, and Emotions." Philos Trans R Soc Lond B Biol Sci. 369(1644), 2014. doi: 10.1098/rstb.2013.0175.
51   Denis Paré. "Role of the Basolateral Amygdala in Memory Consolidation." Progress in Neurobiology. 70(5), 2003: 409–20. https://doi.org/10.1016/S0301-0082(03)00104-7.

Having said this, what generally happens with events that trigger high levels of emotions is that we tend to play those memories automatically. We naturally replay the event in our minds to try to make sense of it, to try to work out what we could have done differently (and therefore, what we'll do differently, next time), and because the part of the brain involved in survival can't tell the difference between reality and imagination. So, every time we recall the event, the brain prompts the stress chemicals that create that survival response. And that causes us to focus even more on that event—in order to stay alive, it's more important to focus on the dangerous wild animal than on the pretty flowers.

Of course, a similar thing happens with good experiences, but it's not nearly as intense, and it needs more conscious engagement and effort because it's not part of the emergency survival system. So, when we have a particularly good experience, the brain triggers the production of those "feel-good" chemicals, but since those chemicals don't trigger the state of survival, their impact is not as strong. Good experiences need deliberate repetition for us to remember them in the face of negative experiences. Many people feel they have more negative memories than positive ones. That's because:

1. The negative experiences were accompanied by stress chemicals, and
2. They're more likely to have repeated those negative events in their minds, automatically, firing those neural patterns over and over, which strengthens those connections.

It's all part of the survival system.

And that is why this part of the process of changing negative childhood memories is so important. You're not just *thinking* about the new memories, you are strengthening the neural connections and other memory-storing systems in your brain, which establishes those new memories as "fact." The old negative memories were probably a lot easier to remember because they automatically and unconsciously put your brain and body into a state of survival.

RECAP:

- Everything we experience is based on the information stored (our memories) from previous experiences. Most of the memories that "prove" who we are and how the world works (implicit memories) are formed in childhood. This is the reason we change childhood memories—the "roots of the weed"—rather than memories of adult experiences (the stem, leaves, and branches of the weed that we can currently see).

- Not only *can* memories be changed, but they're *already* changing and being updated, every time we recall them.

- To change a negative memory, you just need to imagine it differently and then repeat it over and over, just as you would learn a new phone number. What makes the difference is the associated emotions (stress chemicals) involved, so you must first bring those stress chemicals down before you're able to imagine the event differently. Adding positive emotions (feel-good chemicals) will help your brain to prioritize establishing that new memory more quickly and effectively.

- In order to establish the new memories, you need to repeat them over and over—with the good emotions that go with them (love, connection, fun, feeling safe). This will help your brain to establish the new neural networks.

Special Note:

Being creative and imaginative is helpful in the process of strengthening a new positive memory. Remind yourself that there are no memory police (no one even needs to know you're doing this—you are the boss of your own brain and how you choose to fire those neurons!). And there is no limit to the budget or special effects inside your own mind so add exciting and fun detail and make the new memory as wonderful as you can. The more fabulous you make the new memory, the stronger the "feel-good" chemicals, and the more evidence you're providing for your brain that *proves* the results you want to experience in your life, moving forward!

Chapter 6

What if You Tried it Now?

> *"Rather than a memory being permanently stored forever, after it's been learned, actually, memories are far more dynamic than that. And they go through these repeated rounds of going into a state where they can be modified and updated, and then being restored in the brain in that updated form."*
> —Dr. Amy Milton[52]

Learning this information is an empowering start but experiencing it firsthand is what will really turbo-boost your progress! Choose a negative memory to change, right now. Nothing traumatic (be sure to get help from a professional therapist or practitioner when addressing any trauma)—just something that you wish had happened differently. If you have a memory from childhood, great, if not it can be a memory from any time in your life.

As you read the following example, follow along with Odille to address and change your own negative memory.

52   "Editing Memories." Futureproof with John McCrea. August 1, 2020. Podcast. https://www. newstalk.com/podcasts/futureproof-with-jonathan-mccrea/editing-memories.

An example from Odille:

I had a memory of something my mother had told me about. I didn't have a memory of the event itself, but as we're told about experiences by others, the brain forms a memory as if we had been there. Especially when (as is the case, here) the story is told to us repeatedly. My mum would tell me about this, as a cute anecdote, and I'd never thought about it as a "bad" memory until my sister pointed out the significance of it.

My mum was distraught. I was around two years old at the time, and my two baby siblings—twins—were around six months old. Our dad wasn't around, he was working most of the time, and she was alone with the three of us, in a new country, without her family, and over-whelmed. The babies were crying non-stop, and she had reached the end of her tether. (Not so amusing so far, is it?) She was crying and banging on the wall in complete despair. She looked down (here's the "cute" part of the story, the reason she shared it), and there was little two-year-old me, standing next to her, copying her—banging on the wall in the same way she was.

As I said, my mum told this story as a cute, funny anecdote, and that's how I heard and understood it, with a clear image in my mind of that scene. No negative emotions. Years later, however, my sister pointed out the intensity of that experience, not just for our mum, but for that little me.

To the survival part of the brain, as children, when our caregivers aren't happy, we aren't safe. As humans, we are completely reliant on—and at the mercy of—those around us, during our infant and childhood years. Therefore, when those caregivers are upset, angry, hurt, wor-ried, or in any other negative state, the brain of the child immediately registers life-threatening danger and produces stress chemicals, putting the brain and body into that emergency state.

The little me would have been in that emergency state while copying my mother. Banging on the wall—while it may have looked cute—would have been that child's way of trying to help, and/or learning how to survive from observing and then copying her mother. Whatever the little me was experiencing in that moment it would definitely not have involved "feel-good" chemicals.

Moving forward, my life was very much one of stress and I followed in my mum's footsteps regarding her levels of stress and emotional triggers—including feeling unbearably upset whenever she was upset. As teenagers, my siblings and I each reacted to our mother's stress differently. Whenever my mum (a single parent from when we were still little) would get into those states of despair, I would cry with her, feeling the pain I thought she was feeling; my sister would become angry with her, seeing her emotional outbursts as manipulative; my brother would walk in with: "Mum, can I get a lift to Westville?"

Those three completely different responses to our mum's emotional struggles represent three completely different coping skills: same family, same overall circumstances, but vastly different internal experiences for each child, automatically creating different references, resulting in different coping skills.

My automatic response was to join my mum, to feel her feelings and want to help her by getting into the pit of despair with her. My sister's response was the "fight" part of the freeze-flight-fight emergency response. The unconscious part of her brain referred to references for being manipulated—her way of not being sucked into the despair was to get angry and fight it. Our brother (my sister's twin) developed a different coping mechanism—he would automatically and unconsciously distance himself from the emotions completely (dissociation), and change the subject, behaving as if there was nothing going on at all. This, of course, came across as unfeeling and uncaring (I remember thinking he was "resilient" and referring to his reactions as "water off a duck's back"). It would amp up the emotional drama and suffering in both our mum and me. But the truth is, the damage in him was deep, and the coping skill his brain had automatically come up with—the only way of "surviving" trauma (there was more to our story than our mum's emotional despair, of course)—was to dissociate.

So, back to that original memory of the story my mum told me, about two-year-old me, copying her banging on the wall in despair. Since this wasn't a trauma memory, although it must have been traumatic at the time, I didn't have strong negative emotions associated with it, so it's a good example to use for this test. Some negative emotions were introduced to it when I realized the truth of that experience, from what my sister pointed out. So, here's the process as I did it. You can follow along, as you read this, aiming at a memory of your own:

1. I started by taking a deep breath, closing my eyes, and thinking of my favorite color (purple). I imagined being surrounded by that beautiful color and allowed myself to focus on the feeling of that gorgeous shade of purple.

2. I imagined hugging my "subject" (my son when he was a baby) and allowed myself to fully feel that wonderful sensation of love.

3. I imagined that feeling as a ball of light, spreading down to my toes, up to the top of my head, and out to my fingertips.

4. Once that good feeling was strong, I imagined "pressing pause" on it and went to the memory of little two-year-old me, with my mum, both banging on the wall in despair. And I noticed how strong the negative emotions were in that

memory, zero to 10. Although it wasn't strong, there was still some negative feeling there—around a five.

5. As soon as I noticed it, I immediately imagined "pressing pause" on it, going back to the purple and hugging my son. Once that good feeling was strong again, I imagined "pressing pause" on that scene, and returned again to the two-year-old me memory. I asked myself how strong the negative feelings were now. It was a five before, is it still the same? Is it more? Less? It was around a three. (It's very important not to spend time in the negative memory—a couple of seconds is enough to notice how strong the negative emotions are).

6. I did this back and forth, until I went to the two-year-old me memory and there were no negative emotions. I could still see the scene, but there were no emotions.

7. Then, I imagined it differently. I imagined that, instead of my mum and I banging on the wall in despair, we were dancing. And the story my mum told me was that she and my dad (see, what I did there? I put my dad in the picture, even though he wasn't in the original event!) were dancing. They were playing music (I see a record player—you could add a specific song, but I didn't need that detail, I just know there was fun music playing) and doing a funny dance, laughing together. And then they looked down (that's from my mum looking down to see me, in the original memory), and there was little two-year-old me, copying their dance moves. And that, of course, is the "copying my mum" from the original memory. Now that memory is genuinely cute and funny and has a wonderful feeling of fun, safety, connection, and love—instead of despair.

8. I practiced that new memory until it felt strong and real.

As I changed these memories of my mum being distraught and in despair (the memories I had from experiences, as well as those she told me about) to the opposite, positive, and empowering, my deep pain on behalf of my mum, the empath in me, the suffering, all of that diminished and was replaced with love That shift completely changed not only my own emotional patterns, but also my relationship with my mum. It transformed the relationship so that I was kind, compassionate, and supportive, instead of suffering with her and trying to make her change so that I wouldn't be in pain anymore. Empowerment, compassion, kindness, and unconditional love replaced pain, suffering, helplessness, and despair.

RECAP:

As you go through the process of changing your negative childhood memories to the opposite, positive, and empowering, it's important to keep reminding yourself:

- Memories are not permanent and are already changing.
- There are no people or events inside your brain. There are just neurons connecting, and you get to decide to change how those neurons are connecting.
- As you change your implicit childhood memories, you will still remember what originally happened, but it will no longer be "proving" negative beliefs.
- The unconscious part of your brain cannot tell the difference between reality and imagination, cannot use logic or reason, and cannot judge something as unrealistic. It will believe whatever you give it. Just as it believes a movie is real (and triggers a physiological response you experience as an emotion) while you know, consciously, that it's just a movie.

You have complete control over what you change. You are the only boss of your own memories, your own brain. You get to decide which data you keep, which data you change (and into what), and which neurons to fire in what pattern.

Although changing those GPS coordinates from where you are now to where you want to be is as simple as bringing down the emotions and then imagining the memory differently, it's not always easy. The fact that stress chemicals that create negative emotions are stronger than "feel-good" chemicals (for survival) can make it challenging to "stay on the road." The next section of this book will help you to get through the challenges and detours, so that you can reach your destination sooner.

Pillar Three

STAYING ON THE ROAD— ZERO TOLERANCE

Chapter 7

Storms and Detours

An example from Odille:

Up until 2016, when I was trying to change my financial patterns of struggle, my desired "end destination" was to have more than enough money to pay my bills. As long as I kept my focus on the feeling of financial abundance, I was "heading toward my destination."

But then I would receive an unexpected bill that I couldn't pay—a "storm along the road to my destination." I would take that bill as a sign that what I was doing wasn't working and would feel despondent. I would see it as "going backwards" and it would trigger me. I would feel hopeless and that there was no point in even trying anymore. That would be me heading "off-road" into the wilderness. Into the dark, rough terrain of where I didn't want to be. Where the storm continued to rage. And the longer I wandered around in that wilderness, the more off-course I would get. And there would come a time (and it doesn't take long) when I would get so far from the road, that I would no longer be able to see it, and all I could see was the darkness, and no sign of the road to my destination...

Don't Get Out of the Car

Knowing how to drive and having the GPS coordinates set to match the intended destination is only effective if we stay on the road. If, every time we hit a storm or a detour, we pull over, get out of the car, and spend time in that storm or detour—as if it's all there is—we'll never reach our destination.

It's important to recognize that it's natural to focus on the bad stuff. It's part of our survival system. So, whenever the brain registers "danger," it's designed to ignore everything else. You don't want to take your eyes off that bear, because if you do, you may no longer be around to appreciate the pretty flowers!

> *"We inherited the genes that predispose us to give special attention to those negative aspects of our environments that could be harmful to us."*
> —Timothy J. Bono, Ph.D.[53]

When we encounter "storms" along the road, the storm is all we can see at that time. It looks like the whole world is in a storm since we can't see beyond it from where we are. Our natural tendency is to assume that we won't ever reach our destination, and so we "buy into" the experience of the storm being all there is. In other words: When we encounter challenges to what we want along the way, we automatically "buy into them" and, depending on our own particular self-image and worldview from childhood references, we react accordingly.

For example: Jenny is practicing the exercise for controlling her brain chemistry. She's changed her negative childhood memories to positive and empowering ones, and is practicing those new memories, and keeping her focus on what she wants. What she wants is more money, since she's currently only just scraping by.

---

53   Margaret Jaworski. "The Negativity Bias: Why the Bad Stuff Sticks," Psycom, https://www.psy-com.net/negativity-bias. Accessed October 10, 2021.

So, she's on the road, focusing on her goals, and she's checked that the coordinates in her "GPS" (childhood memories) match that destination of having more than enough. And then, a "storm" hits. She receives an unexpected bill that means she has to go into overdraft or borrow money. Naturally, this triggers her—she was doing so well, she was focusing on her destination and making sure her GPS matched that destination. Now, however, she's "gone backwards."

Or has she?

It's a matter of perception and the meaning we automatically assign to what we experience. Jenny will naturally feel emotionally triggered at first, but it's what she chooses to do from there that will determine her results.

Option One:

If (like most of us) Jenny stays in that triggered state, and "buys into" the feeling of: *It's not working. Why does this always happen to me? Nothing's changed*, and other similar thoughts, that's like pulling over, getting out of the car, and fully focusing on being in that storm. How bad it is, how inconvenient it is, and how much it's keeping her from her end destination.

As Jenny's brain continues to fire neurons in those particular patterns (negative thoughts), her limbic system is, in real time, pumping more and more stress chemicals into her brain and body. And as those stress chemicals continue to impact her brain and body, part of that response is blood draining from the part of her brain she needs for cognitive thinking.

This results in a vicious circle of negative thoughts and negative feelings, which means she's unable to find solutions or see options and opportunities and so she stays stuck in that storm. Of course, it's practically impossible to keep your focus on the lovely end destination when you're dealing with the "bear" in front of you.

Option Two:

If Jenny can recognize the "storm" as *just* a storm along the way to her end destination she will be able to keep moving forward through it, instead of getting out and pitching a tent. She may have to slow down a bit, visibility may deteriorate, she may feel frightened, but she will be able to keep reminding herself that it's only a storm on her journey, not an alternative end destination. And if the storm is particularly scary, she may put on the radio, music, or an uplifting audio book, or call a friend who will talk her through the storm. But she will keep moving toward her desired destination.

In other words, when she sees that unexpected bill, and when she realizes the implications of it, she'll be able to remind herself that it doesn't "mean" anything other than the meaning she gives it. She can choose to see it as a "storm" along the road, and she can choose to not buy into it. She can remind herself to keep her focus on her end destination (financial freedom) and maintain control of her vehicle (do whatever it takes to keep her focus on what feels good—to keep the stress chemicals down, the "feel-good" chemicals high, and her cognitive thinking online). She can check those GPS coordinates (play the new childhood memories with all their associated good feelings) to make sure they're all in alignment with that end destination and change any that aren't.

And as she does this, she keeps control of her vehicle and stays on the road: Her prefrontal cortex stays online, which means she has full access to her cognitive thinking and is able to think clearly, problem-solve, and see opportunities she couldn't have seen while triggered.

An example from Odille continued:

Once I got that far off the road and lost in the wilderness of negative emotions, it would be almost impossible to find my way back to the road again. Because now, surrounded by the darkness, with no sign of a road, the doubts would kick in. What road? There is no road. And so, I would continue to wander around, lost in that dark wilderness.

If, on the other hand, I was applying Zero Tolerance, which means having no tolerance for any negative thought or feeling, no matter how small and apparently harmless, I'd be able to catch that detour before I got too far from the road. When the storm hit (the unexpected bill turned up, or I lost income, or I didn't get the job I'd hoped for), I'd remind myself that it's just a storm, and that, as long as I stay on the road and keep facing the direction of my destination, I'll eventually come out of that storm. If I did end up facing a different direction and heading into the wilderness, as soon as I was aware of it I would turn around and get back on the road. And it would be much easier and quicker because I wouldn't be that far from it.

An example from a client:

In one of our daily group sessions, Susan, an 18-year-old, shared her struggles with anxiety, her fear of failing exams, and being rejected by medical school.

May 18th, 2020

"I've been feeling anxiety regarding an application outcome that is coming out this week. I can't seem to change memories of the feeling I have of opening an email regarding previous application outcomes. The anxiety is so strong that it's really hard."

May 21, 2020

"I got rejected from medical school yesterday, yet again... Others around me keep getting more and more medical school offers, and I keep getting rejected. I have feelings of being left out."

We helped Susan deal with a range of challenges, including feeling inadequate. We guided her through changing plenty of negative childhood memories and using the Due Justice Technique (Chapter 15), the Allowing Technique (Chapter 17), and Touchstones (Chapter 18). Over time, as she changed her childhood memories, practiced the new ones, and continued to practice the Beginner's Exercise from Chapter 2, her anxiety reduced, she started thinking differently, and was able to achieve A*AA (exceeding the required AAA score) on her final exams, allowing her to apply to medical school despite her original lack of confidence in herself.

Email on February 1st, 2021
"ODILLE...I'M A MEDICAL STUDENT!! I got into one of my universities!"

However, during February and March, despite getting into one of the universities on her list, she realized she had a powerful fear of being rejected by her first-choice university and ending up at one that didn't appeal to her.

We changed more childhood memories, and once again used the Allowing Technique and Touchstones.

Email on March 31st, 2021
"ODILLE, YOU WILL NOT BELIEVE IT...

I'M A MEDICAL STUDENT PART 2...

Ahhhh...

I'm so grateful—I just found out that I got into my top choice university!

I'm crying, shaking, and I'm so grateful for you."

RECAP:

- The brain has a "negative bias"—we're designed to focus on the "danger" for survival.
- Negative thoughts trigger stress chemicals, causing negative emotions, which in turn trigger more negative thoughts—and so the negative cycle is perpetuated.
- Since stress chemicals are stronger than "feel-good chemicals," the earlier you change your focus (switch off the stress chemical tap and switch on the "feel-good" chemical tap) the easier it will be to change your emotional state.

It's Not Always Easy

When things look like they're not going to work out, or you can't see how you'll get where you want to be, from where you currently are, it's not always easy to choose your focus. Because, unfortunately, it's easier to feel bad, than to feel good.

Why it's Easier to Feel Bad

It's easier to feel bad than to feel good. That's part of being human, and it's part of our survival system. The effects of stress chemicals[54] on the body are far more powerful than the effects of "feel-good" chemicals, because ultimately, they keep us alive. And this means that the higher the level of those stress chemicals, the more difficult it is to switch from feeling bad to feeling good. Add to this the fact that stress chemicals cause blood to drain from the cognitive-thinking part of your brain and you can see how easy it is to get stuck in a loop of negative feelings, causing negative thoughts... causing more negative feelings, with no way to see solutions and options that would break that pattern.

> *"In effect, the brain is like Velcro for negative experiences, but Teflon for positive ones. That shades "implicit memory"—your underlying expectations, beliefs, action strategies, and mood— in an increasingly negative direction."*
>
> —Rick Hanson[55], Ph.D, psychologist, and Senior Fellow of the Greater Good Science Center at UC Berkeley, and *New York Times* best-selling author

---

54 Anil Kumar, Puneet Rinwa, Gurleen Kaur, & Lalit Machawal. "Stress: Neurobiology, Consequences and Management." J Pharm Bioallied Sci. 5(2), 2013:91–97. doi:10.4103/0975-7406.111818. https://www.ncbi.nlm.nih.gov/pmc/articles/PMC3697199/.
55 Rick Hanson, "Take in the Good." The Practical Science of Lasting Happiness. www.rickhanson.net/take-in-the-good/.

When the Mind Has a Mind of its Own

Timothy had made great progress with changing childhood memories of abuse. We'd helped him to create a new childhood timeline, filled with love, safety, connection, and fun. He was already experiencing changes in his relationship with his wife and feeling more positive about life and his future. However, he was still dealing with intense anxiety around his job and his boss. He told us that he was finding it impossible to control his chemical state using the Beginner's Exercise. He couldn't seem to pull himself out of the negative spiral, no matter what he tried.

It turned out that whenever Timothy felt his anxiety triggered by thinking about his job, he would immediately start to think of the last confrontation he had with his boss. That would increase the anxiousness and lead to more negative thoughts—worries about what would happen the next time he made a mistake, and fears of getting fired. And those thoughts amped up the fear and anxiety further, which, in turn, led to more rumination about what would happen if he couldn't find another job... And so, the momentum continued.

This is why we use Zero Tolerance. The earlier you switch off the "hot water tap" (neural connections that trigger stress chemicals) and switch on the "cold water tap" (neural connections that trigger "feel-good" chemicals) the easier it will be, since the level of hot water (stress chemicals) won't be as high, and your prefrontal cortex will still be online, enabling you to think clearly.

Remember, it only takes 60 to 90 seconds to change your chemical state (and therefore your emotional state) from stress chemicals to "feel-good" chemicals—as long as you keep your focus off the negative and on the positive. The sooner you start shifting your focus (firing a different pattern of neurons), the easier it will be to keep your focus off the negative for that minute and a half.

If you saw one small cockroach in your home, you wouldn't say to yourself, *"Ah, it's only one, and it's only a small one,"* and leave it there. You'd do something about it, immediately, and you'd want to make sure there weren't others. Because if you allowed that one small cockroach to continue living in your home, you know there would be more. Negative thoughts are the same. One small negative thought—if not addressed— will lead to others.

You can think of them as cockroaches or remind yourself of the physiology behind it—that every moment you're giving space to a nega- tive thought (even if it's just one small one) you're pumping stress chemi- cals into your system—and those chemicals are stronger than "feel-good" chemicals. That means that with just one small thought you are setting a momentum that can quickly overcome you and make it exponentially more difficult to pull yourself out of that negative state. In every moment, the effects of those stress chemicals multiply—and much more quickly than you might expect.

You can also think of this negativity spiral as a "slippery slope." No matter how much you think you can control your footing, as you step onto it, you will start to slide, and the further you allow yourself to slide, the faster and further you go, and the less chance you have of being able to stop.

We asked Timothy what happened inside his mind when he thought about work, and his reply was that he felt fear. He was afraid of confronta- tion and his boss was stressed, overwhelmed, and quick to snap. In addition to changing his negative childhood memories and practicing the new ones, we suggested that Timothy practice Zero Tolerance by becoming aware of his thoughts and addressing any negative ones as soon as he noticed them.

We are always moving forward—and this is significant—*in the direc- tion we're facing at the time.* Think of your life as a vehicle that you are driving: You've learned how to drive (controlling your brain chemistry). You've changed the GPS coordinates to match the destination you want to end up in. Now it's about staying on the road. Whichever direction you're facing—at that moment—is the direction in which you are moving. If you're facing the destination you want to end up in, that's the direction you're heading in, at that moment. If you're facing the scenery on the side of the road, or the destination you don't want to end up in, that's the direction you're heading in, at that moment.

In other words, while you are focusing on feeling the way you want to feel, you're traveling in the direction of more of that feeling. So, when you focus on the things you're worried about, on betrayal, on regret, you're moving in the direction of more worry, more betrayal, more regret.

As you can imagine, the longer you face in a particular direction that's not your desired destination, the longer it takes to get back on the road that leads to that destination. And it's okay to turn around at any point and head in the right direction—it just may be more difficult and take longer to do so if you've been travelling on the wrong road for a while.

Therefore, the sooner you become aware you're wandering off-road and into the wilderness, the easier it will be to get back en route. If you catch it early enough, you'll still be able to see the road from where you are. If not, you may find yourself doubting that you'll find the road again because you can't see it from so far away. In other words, when the negative emotions have become very intense and you've had those stress chemicals in your system for a long time, you may not be able to see any hope—any sign of how to achieve the changes you want in your life. It takes faith that, if you start heading in the *direction* of the road, even though you can't see it yet (focusing on the positive), and get increasingly closer to the road (lowering the level of stress chemicals), you'll start to see it more clearly, and then it will become easier to continue heading back toward it.

This is where Zero Tolerance comes in. It is about developing awareness and having "zero tolerance" for any negative thoughts—no matter how small or fleeting or whether there are negative emotions yet, or not.

Odille's introduction to Zero Tolerance

I did a lot of wandering around the dark wilderness, unable to remember there even was a road, never mind finding a way to get back to it. But the day I created this technique, I realized the power of it. From then on, I decided to use Zero Tolerance for any negative thought or feeling, no matter how small. I created it after discovering that one negative thought or feeling can seem "innocent" but because stress chemicals are so much stronger than we think, they can run away with us before we've had a chance to realize what's happening.

It was late December 2015. I was "facing the direction I wanted to go"—in other words, focusing on staying in a state of feeling good, changing childhood memories, and practicing the new ones. And as I was doing some chores around the house, I noticed a small, fleeting thought: "I don't know how I'm going to pay the gas bill." Seems harmless enough, right? Only a small thought, it had zipped in and out of my head before I'd even registered it. And, in fact, because it was so little and harmless, and because I didn't feel any negative emotions with it, I thought it was small enough to ignore. But because I had, just that morning, decided on this idea of "Zero Tolerance" I stopped, and said to myself, "If we're doing Zero Tolerance, we're doing Zero Tolerance."

I treated it as one small cockroach—apparently innocent, but definitely a sign of more to come. So, I said to myself: "Okay, I don't know how I'm going to pay the gas bill.

QUESTION: What's wrong with that? (ANSWER: They'll be angry with me.)
QUESTION: And what will happen then? (ANSWER: I'll get demand letters.)
QUESTION: And what will I do then? (ANSWER: I don't know.)

QUESTION: And what's wrong with not knowing? (ANSWER: It's scary not knowing.)

QUESTION: And where, in my childhood, did I have this feeling of being scared and not knowing? (ANSWER: Too many times to count.)

And in that moment, I created new childhood memories of my grandparents and my mum, smiling and explaining things (I didn't need to know what those things were, I just imagined them explaining something) kindly and patiently, and then asking me—kindly and patiently— "Any questions?" And since, in my family, asking questions was a trigger for those stressed adults, I imagined that "Any questions?" became a family catchphrase. Something they always asked, in a fun, humorous way, but that they then always honored and answered any questions we asked.

That gas bill was still there. I still didn't know how I would pay it, but I hadn't wandered off into the wilderness. I was still "on the road." I felt calm, safe, and loved, instead of helpless, hopeless, and frightened. Feeling that way didn't magically make the bill disappear, or mean I suddenly had the money to pay it. But neither would languishing in helplessness, hopelessness, fear, and despair. What feeling calm, safe, and loved did do was keep my prefrontal cortex online so that I was able to think clearly, and access my problem-solving skills, risk assessment, creative thinking, and judgment. I put the bill aside for the time being, but this time, not to avoid it or out of fear. I decided that as I couldn't pay it right away, I would play those new childhood memories until a solution automatically came to me.

The next morning, I came up with an idea that was obvious, but I had never thought of before. That idea eventually led to an increase in my income, which not only allowed me to pay that gas bill, and all my other bills, but also allowed me to travel internationally several times the following year.

Now, because I had caught that very first thought of, "I don't know how I'm going to pay the gas bill" early, the level of stress chemicals in my system wasn't high yet. In fact, the reason I almost ignored the thought was because there were no negative feelings associated with it. But that is also what made it so easy to change. If I had ignored it, it would have led to more thoughts in the background: "I don't have the money to pay it... I'm going to get into trouble... Why hasn't this changed yet?... Why do I always end up struggling?... What am I going to do?... I can't believe I'm still in this position even after all the work I've done..." And every one of those neural connections, would have caused my brain to automatically produce stress chemicals that would have quickly overwhelmed any "feel-good" chemicals. Blood would have drained from my prefrontal cortex, and I would have ended up in the familiar vicious cycle of negative thoughts and feelings, wandering around in the dark wilderness of helplessness, hopelessness, and despair. All from ignoring one very small "cockroach." All from ignoring one small, apparently harmless thought.

RECAP:

- Negative thoughts and feelings are like cockroaches—no matter how small and apparently harmless they may be on their own, they are sure to be a sign of more to come.
- The earlier you address the first negative thought or feeling you notice—and switch your focus—the easier it will be to get back on the road to your desired destination.
- Remember, it takes only 60 to 90 seconds to change your brain and body chemistry from stress chemicals to "feel-good" chemicals—as long as you keep your focus off the negative and on the positive for that 60 to 90 seconds.

The tricky part is becoming aware of those habitual unconscious negative thoughts that have become so automatic, we no longer notice them. If we don't see the "cockroach" we can't deal with it.

What if there were a way for you to close the gate that automatically allows those negative thoughts in, in the first place?

Chapter 9

Close the Gate

Catching that first, small "cockroach" (negative thought) can be challenging—especially if it blends into the carpet. Learning what signs to look out for will give you the opportunity to prevent that cockroach from inviting its friends and family to move in! Gateway Thoughts are what we call these little, apparently harmless negative thoughts that you don't normally notice or pay attention to.

They are habitual thoughts that seem harmless but usually lead to more and more dangerous thoughts: *I don't know what to do…* Or, *I just can't do this.* Or, *Why do I always____?* Or, *I should have…*

Gateway Thoughts may be little—and you may usually ignore them—but one, like cockroaches, will inevitably lead to more.

You can gain control over Gateway Thoughts—lowering the frequency and intensity of becoming emotionally triggered—using Zero Tolerance.

Zero Tolerance means becoming aware of—and having zero tolerance for—*any* negative thoughts. It means addressing those thoughts before they lead to that slippery slope. Before that one small "cockroach" brings its friends and family into your home. It's about getting into the habit of closing that gate as soon as you notice it's open—before all the other negative thoughts can rush through too, with all the stress chemicals that come with them.

This is not about ignoring negative thoughts and feelings—it's about *answering* them. Acknowledging them and addressing them, in the moment, before they lead to more.

What to Do with Gateway Thoughts

1. Practice becoming aware of your own Gateway Thoughts—we've listed some examples you can look out for below.
2. When you notice a Gateway Thought, catch yourself immediately and address it. It's within your control to turn it around (even though it appears to be true in the moment).
3. Play a new childhood memory of your parents reassuring you.

Note from Steve

I believe that Gateway Thoughts are linked to implicit memory and the beliefs that we have ended up creating about ourselves and our place in the world. I also believe that they are about habit and creating that normal "at-home" feeling or emotional state. As I initially began working on finding and changing implicit childhood memories, I discovered the theme, or pattern, of being a victim. I have memories from early on of knowing that our family had a long history of painful failures, loss, and plenty of examples of being denied opportunities and being taken advantage of by those in a more powerful position.

As a child, I remember spending time at my grandmother's house. I used to stop on my way home from school and spend time just sitting with her and listening to her stories. I didn't recognize it at the time, of course, but I was showing up for my daily dose of learning who I was within this particular family, how this family saw itself in the larger world, and how all of that felt.

My grandmother would tell me stories of her family moving from Central Illinois to South Dakota to try their hand at homesteading.

How they had lost a little brother to illness and had eventually lost the farm after three years of bad weather. I heard about various illnesses she had dealt with over the years, how she'd had her dreams cut short by the loss of her mother at an early age and been left with the responsibility of raising her younger sister. Being at my grandmother's house had a particular feel to it, and I now see that I came to associate it with my "at-home" feeling of who I was, how the world worked, and my place within it.

From the stories that I heard on a near daily basis during a very impressionable time in my life, I learned that I had come from a long line of unfortunate people who were at the mercy of circumstance, the weather, bad luck, people with more power and money, and physical illness. We were victims. And because my father had also been raised in this environment and belief system, my own family home took on a similar feeling. This feeling was home—being a victim felt like home.

I feel that Gateway Thoughts are there to help us return to that "at-home" feeling when we encounter something new or are feeling unsure in the moment. Even though this feeling may not necessarily be a positive one, it's what we know and what our unconscious mind has linked to safety. So, as I began to change my own childhood memories and the stories of my ancestral family (a process we will discuss later) I found that certain Gateway Thoughts would emerge, automatically.

I had been living in this "home" for so long that everything was geared to feeling this way. As I began to make changes, however, my life began to feel different, and this of course clashed with the old "at-home" feeling. It's like moving to a new house or apartment—it takes a little while of living there before it feels like home.

Becoming aware of Gateway Thoughts and using Zero Tolerance helps to establish the new "at-home" feeling. So, I began to call out any thought or feeling of victimhood as soon as I noticed it (sometimes audibly) and remind myself: That was the old story… You are no longer a victim, and I would immediately replay new childhood memories and stories of my amazing family that felt like the new "at home" of empowerment.

Examples of Gateway Thoughts

- I should have…
- Why didn't I…?
- I don't know what to do.
- Why do I always…?
- Why do they always…?
- How am I supposed to…?
- What will they think?

RECAP:

- Gateway Thoughts are habitual negative thoughts that appear to be harmless, but will always be followed by more negative thoughts, which will eventually trigger stress chemicals.
- The longer you allow yourself to go along with these negative thoughts, the more difficult it can be to find your way back to feeling good again.

It's not always easy to notice these thoughts since they're habitual—we're so used to them that we are often completely unaware of them. That's where Rumble Strips come in!

Rumble Strips

f you've ever driven on a highway, you may have experienced the shock of being jolted out of calmly drifting toward the shoulder by what sounds like your vehicle falling apart under you.

Rumble strips are grooves along the edge of a road that cause a vibration and loud noise when the tires of a vehicle go over them. The strips are there to grab the driver's attention so they're able to steer their vehicle back to the middle of their lane before they end up careering off the road.

When you start to feel a negative emotion—before it becomes strong—that's you hitting the Rumble Strip. It's the warning that you're about to head off the road.

> *"Emotions drive behavior. Every decision is*
> *an emotional decision at some level."*
>
> —James Clear[56]

While you're focused on your desired destination and enjoying the journey—keeping yourself in a state of feeling good and making sure your GPS is in alignment with what you want to experience in your life—you're

---

56   James Clear. (2016). *Atomic Habits: An Easy & Proven Way to Build Good Habits & Break Bad Ones.* (New York, NY: Avery).

on the road toward that destination. When you start to feel a negative emotion, you're hitting the rumble strip on the side of that road. If you ignore the rumble strip and keep focusing on that negative thought, leading to more negative thoughts and more stress chemicals, and taking your prefrontal cortex offline, you will head off-road, either into the wilderness or back in the direction you came from.

How long you stay in an emotionally triggered state will determine how far you wander off-road, and therefore how long it will take to get back on that road again. You can turn around and head back to the road at any point, but the earlier you make that choice, of course, the quicker and easier it will be to get back on track. And those Rumble Strips will help you to catch yourself before you come off the road completely.

Examples of Rumble Strips

- Feeling slightly irritable
- Starting to feel overwhelmed
- Feeling a little anxious
- Starting to feel frustrated
- A background feeling of sadness or melancholy

As soon as you notice you're not feeling good, remind yourself that you've hit the Rumble Strip and do what you can to correct your steering:

- Look for five things to be grateful for
- Imagine being surrounded by your favorite color
- Imagine hugging someone or something you love
- Do some physical exercise

Then play a new childhood memory. If you can't manage to change your focus, use the Allowing Technique in Chapter 17.

Remember: It only takes 60 to 90 seconds to change your brain and body chemistry from stress chemicals to "feel-good" chemicals (from negative emotions to positive ones) as long as you keep your focus off the negative and on the positive for that full minute and a half.

You have control over that "switch," even though it really doesn't feel like it. And as long as you keep that "switch" flipped to "feel-good" chemicals (in other words, keeping your focus on something you love or are grateful for, or are looking forward to—or even just focusing on your favorite color) you will physically be stopping the production of stress chemicals and instead triggering the flow of "feel-good" chemicals in your brain and body.

And, as we've pointed out, the earlier you catch it and "flick that switch," the easier and quicker the process will be. The longer you allow those stress chemicals to flood your bloodstream, the more difficult it can be to change your focus—that's the survival mechanism.

RECAP:

- Just as rumble strips on the freeway warn you that you're about to drive your vehicle off the road, the first signs of negative feelings (before they become strong) are warning you that you're starting to pump stress chemicals into your system.
- Just as you would correct your steering to prevent your vehicle from continuing over the rumble strip, off the road, and away from the route to your destination, you can use the techniques in this book to change your focus before the level of stress chemicals gets too high and derails your journey.

But there's an important key to being able to use Zero Tolerance effectively—or not.

How to Use Zero Tolerance

The key to developing the skill of keeping yourself on track toward your goals, no matter what you experience, is to practice keeping on track when you're *not* going through challenges. Or to use our analogy: The key to developing the skill of staying on the road and not veering off into the wilderness when you hit a storm, is to practice your driving skills when you're in *clear weather*.

The more you practice this skill, the easier it will become and, most importantly, the more you'll remember to use it!

"Learning allows us to transcend our genes."
—Joseph LeDoux[57]

Zero Tolerance Steps

1. Notice the negative thought or feeling and remind yourself that no matter how small or harmless it seems, it's like seeing one small cockroach—if you allow it to run around, unchecked, it will bring its friends and family.

---

57   Joseph LeDoux. (2003). Synaptic Self: How Our Brains Become Who We Are. (New York, NY: Penguin Books).

2. Answer that small thought or feeling using logic rather than emotions. Ask yourself: What would I say to a friend who was feeling this way or said these words? What would I say to a child I'd adopted (who'd had the same childhood I had), who was expressing this feeling or thought? When you have an answer, say the same to yourself.

3. Choose your focus in that moment. "Flick the switch" from stress chemicals to "feel-good" chemicals in that moment. Start with thinking of your favorite color. Imagine being surrounded by that beautiful color and allow yourself to fully focus on and appreciate how beautiful that color is. If you can't imagine a color in that moment, find a color in your surroundings to focus on.

4. Every time your mind wanders (and it will), just gently bring it back to that color. Reassure yourself that you *will* address the issues, but later, once you've changed your chemical state. You're not ignoring them. You're just getting your cognitive thinking back online to allow yourself to be able to strategize and problem-solve.

Think of your mind as a puppy that hasn't been house-trained yet. Every time the puppy goes to pee on the floor, you need to calmly pick him up and put him outside.

One of the keys to success in house-training the puppy is realizing that he will go to pee on the floor. And when you take him outside, you know that he's probably going to try to pee on the floor again—and again—until he's fully trained. Getting angry and frustrated with the puppy doesn't change anything. In fact, it may make the puppy more stressed, which means he may take longer to become house-trained because his brain will go into survival mode in response to your angry, frustrated reaction and be incapable of making those new neural connections.

Of course, you'll also need to be vigilant and notice as soon as the puppy looks like he's going to pee on the floor so that you can immediately pick him up and put him outside. The longer you wait, the more mess you'll have to clean up.

Your mind is the same. The calmer you are in gently bringing your mind back to that beautiful color, the easier it will be to make those new neural connections. And the earlier you catch it the less "mess" you'll need to clean up, which means the quicker and easier you'll be able to change your chemical (and therefore, your emotional) state.

5. Play one or more new childhood memories. The Bookmark Memories in Chapter 13 are very effective for this purpose.

An example from Odille:

As I write this, Mother's Day was last Sunday, here in the USA. Last Thursday, Steve and I were on our way to visit Steve's parents for an early Mother's Day celebration. I'd cooked a meal, we had flowers and a card for Steve's mother, and we were so looking forward to the evening. Afterward, we were going to see our niece play in the school band for the first time.

Throughout the day, there seemed to be a vague background melancholy. Although it wasn't strong, I (now) knew better than to ignore it. (Step One of Zero Tolerance: Notice the negative thought and remind yourself of Zero Tolerance.)

So, I answered it with: Nothing bad is happening, right now—we're going to have a lovely time at dinner and at the concert when we see everyone. (Step Two of Zero Tolerance: Answer the negative thought or feeling using logic.)

I then chose my focus in that moment—I imagined being surrounded by purple, and I thought of all the things I was looking forward to. (Step Three of Zero Tolerance: Choose your focus.)

The feeling was reduced to neutral, and I mentioned it to Steve. He asked if it's possible that the feeling arose because of the connection of celebrating Mother's Day, and the fact that my own mother had passed away two years ago. He suggested that I imagine we were driving to see my mum for Mother's Day, and instantly I felt a surge of "feel-good" chemicals. Immediately I felt that lift in the way I was feeling.

I knew we weren't going to see my mum—she still died two years ago—but just imagining we were on our way to see her for Mother's Day resulted in my brain triggering "feel-good" chemicals, which completely changed how I was feeling.

Now, if this had all happened in the past, as soon as Steve asked me if my feelings might be about Mother's Day, and even when he suggested that I imagine we were going to see my own mum, I would have allowed my mind to automatically go down the road of regret, pain, and how much I miss her. I would have allowed my mind to focus on the fact that she is no longer here—that I no longer have a mother to celebrate Mother's Day with. I would have allowed my mind to focus on that loss, how sad it is, and how much I wish she were here. I would have allowed my mind to wander off to the "I wish..." and "Why didn't I...?" I would have gone to the memories of not making it in time before she died, and regretting not going earlier, and... All the other negative roads. In other words, I would have allowed that puppy to pee all over the floor before trying to put it outside and clean up the mess. I would have allowed that little cockroach (that vague background feeling of melancholy) to run around and bring its friends (all those negative thoughts and memories of regret, wishing, and longing).

Instead, by catching that "cockroach" or "puppy" immediately, I was able to redirect to the feelings of love, connection, and joy that came with imagining we were going to visit my mum.

Some may see this as delusion, or fooling yourself, but it's no more fooling yourself than watching a movie that triggers an emotional response. Since your conscious mind still knows the original events (I've been able to tell you, here, that my mum died two years ago and that we were on our way to visit Steve's mum), it's only the part of the brain that can't tell the difference between reality and imagination and can't judge something as unrealistic that believes the imaginary scenario. And that's the part of the brain that triggers those chemicals.

When you watch a movie, and you allow yourself to get involved in that movie and feel the emotions it evokes, you aren't fooling yourself or being delusional. You're just allowing yourself to experience those feelings while still knowing, consciously, that it's just a movie.

If I had imagined we were on our way to see my mum, and reminded myself that she's not alive, so we weren't really going to see her, it would have been like sitting through a movie and constantly saying, "But this is not real." There's no need for that, of course (unless it's a scary movie, and you're frightened), and it spoils your experience of the movie.

Who's Taking Who for a Walk?

The unconscious part of your brain is like an untrained dog. The dog has been conditioned through its life experiences to act in specific ways. It doesn't have the ability to think cognitively, reason, and use logic the way we can. Imagine the cortex of your brain is you, and the unconscious part of your brain is the dog. If you want more control over your life experiences, and you have places you want to go and things you want to achieve, you need to gain control over that "dog" because you are always holding the leash with the dog on the other end. And it's a massive dog. If you allow it to start chasing a rabbit, it drags you with it! The key is to use Zero

Tolerance to keep that dog to heel as soon as it starts to show an interest in the rabbit.

Imagine having this big dog with you throughout your day. It's a wonderful dog, and if you train it properly, it will be loyal, protective, loving, and helpful. It will never be able to use reason or logic the way you can, but it's okay—that's your job. And you can work together. If, on the other hand, when the dog starts barking and chasing something or someone that is not a real threat, you "buy into" that behavior and follow the dog, it will keep delaying your results. The techniques we've shared in this book are designed to help you to gain control of that dog, and retrain it, using kindness, compassion, and consistency.

The best part of all of this is that your dog won't listen to anyone else. No one else has any control over your dog. He may *react* to others, but others have no power over him. And you get to retrain him so that he reacts and responds differently. You are the boss. You are the only boss. Even though it may not feel that way sometimes.

Techniques You Can Use for Changing Your Chemical State, in the Moment

- Think of your favorite color and imagine being surrounded by it. Allow yourself to fully focus only on that color and how beautiful it is.
- Look for five things to be grateful for. You don't even need to find any, just the activity of looking for them will start to change your brain chemistry.
- Listen to music you love.
- Imagine yourself as a child, standing in front of you, and imagine hugging that child and reassuring them that you love them.
- Watch uplifting TED Talks.
- Listen to uplifting podcasts.
- Do some physical exercise—even if it's just walking around the block while listening to an uplifting audiobook.
- Do a hobby or other activity you love.

RECAP:

- Wherever you put your focus in the moment determines whether your brain is triggering stress chemicals or "feel-good" chemicals.
- The earlier you change your focus, the easier it is to get back on the right road.
- The unconscious part of your brain is like a puppy—it takes time, patience, and consistency to retrain it, and you can't expect one correction to be all that's needed.

Now, all of this may sound fairly simple and easy to do. However, just like developing any skill or making any changes to the brain and body, there will be resistance, and you will experience ups and downs. That's what the rest of this book is all about.

REST AND REPAIR STOPS— TROUBLE-SHOOTING

Staying Alive

"I can't imagine my mother being affectionate."
"My memory won't change."
"I can't remember my childhood."
"The old memory keeps coming back."
"In my culture, boys have always been more important than girls."
"I just feel too angry—why should they get away with it?"
"I can't get out of the negative emotions spiral."
"It shouldn't have been that way."
"There's just too much to change, I'm overwhelmed."
"I've changed that memory already, but it's still coming up."

As with any road trip, making a few stops along the way is to be expected. Some are planned while others aren't. Sometimes we'll need to refuel, or make a repair, and at other times we may just need a break. Every stop we make along the way, as part of the journey, enables us to continue toward our end destination—the rest or repair stop doesn't replace the destination.

As you start to change negative childhood memories, you may find you're experiencing resistance and challenges. There may be times you can't find a memory, or you can't imagine a parent differently, or you may have doubts, or strong resistance to particular changes. Think of these challenges as warning lights on your car that indicate you need to pull into a rest and repair stop to address that issue before continuing along the route to your end destination. The following chapters will enable you to do that.

The goal is to end up with a whole new childhood that matches and supports (and, in fact, *proves*) whatever it is you want to experience in your life now, moving forward.

As humans, we're not designed to survive alone—we're born completely helpless and reliant on others. Therefore, instinctively, our top priorities are:

1. To be safe
2. To connect with others (which is also part of being safe)

All other priorities, no matter what they are, or what the details are, boil down to these two states of being. These two "drivers" are constantly running in the background, unconsciously, in all our interactions and experiences.

> *"Brains exist because the distribution of resources*
> *necessary for survival and the hazards that*
> *threaten survival vary in space and time."*
> —John Morgan Allman[58]

From birth, the brain is continuously striving to keep us safe, and every experience changes the brain, building a structure—a worldview—of who we are and how the world works, all with the primary goal of being safe.

Part of being "safe" is staying the same. We may not be happy, but we're still alive, right?

---

58   John M. Allman. (1999). Evolving Brains. (New York, NY: Scientific American Library).

So, when we try to change ourselves, it's mostly okay, up to a certain point, but it the change is going to take us too far from that self-image and worldview, we will usually experience resistance.

In the process of getting fit, for example, most people will experience a point at which they are resistant to continuing to work out. Most give up at that point, and it's only those who continue to work out anyway who will overcome that resistance and achieve their fitness goal.

While the consequences of resistance may not make sense to the conscious mind, it's important to remember that the unconscious part of the brain has no ability to use logic or reason.

It's like a guard dog that's conditioned to not let anyone in. That dog has no ability to determine if someone is friendly or not—his automatic reaction is to attack when anyone arrives, no matter who they are. To get the dog to allow a friend into the house, you'd need to recondition him for that particular person. Not by reasoning with him (he won't understand your explanation that this is a close friend), but by reassuring and reconditioning him. There is no logic. Unless the dog is retrained, even if that person arrived with a gift for you and a smile on their face, he would still attack them. If you were sick and they were coming to take you to the hospital, the dog would still attack them. He cannot tell the difference.

That unconscious part of your brain is the same. You may need more money, or be looking for a new relationship, but the unconscious part of your brain has no ability to understand that. All that "guard dog" knows is that if someone tries to enter his house, he attacks. Instinctively, automatically, and with no ability to think it through. In this analogy, the "intruder" represents significant change that your "guard dog," your unconscious brain, will try to resist. If you get too far from who you've always been (and allow the "intruder" in), the unconscious part of your brain will try to bring you back into alignment again. To keep you "safe."

Of course, just like getting frustrated and angry with that guard dog (or even trying to reason with him) won't change his response, it won't change that resistance either.

Through working with hundreds of people (as well as on ourselves), we've developed techniques especially designed for getting past the resistance, and "leveling up" results. Think of these techniques as "rest and repair stops" along the way to your destination.

RECAP:

- Just as with physical fitness and learning a new skill, there is no straight level route from where we are to where we want to be. There are ups and downs and twists and turns in the road—that's just part of the journey.
- The brain's top priority is survival. And part of keeping us alive is keeping us the same as we've always been. Change equals danger. We may not be happy, but we're alive.
- The unconscious part of the brain cannot use logic or reason, so it has no ability to make decisions based on what you want or need—it simply acts according to how it's programmed. In the same way, the color of ink you see on a document is the color that's in the printer. The printer has no ability to change the ink on its own based on your requests.

In Pillar One, you learned to control your vehicle.

In Pillar Two, you learned to change the GPS coordinates to match the destination you're aiming for.

In Pillar Three, you learned to stay on the road when you hit storms or diversions.

On the next stage of your journey, in the following chapters, you'll learn what to do when you experience a flat tire, need the bathroom, or need to refuel.

The Travel Brochure: Bookmark Memories

One of the challenges that many of our clients have faced was that there seemed to be so much to change. While some clients couldn't remember much of their childhood, there were others who had so many memories that it was overwhelming. Where do you start? Which issues do you prioritize? It was like being faced with a pile of puzzle pieces and having no idea what the picture was, or even how many puzzles the pieces belonged to.

The purpose of these Bookmark Memories is to give some guidance and reference for what you're aiming for. When you feel overwhelmed, or don't know where to start or what to do next, keep coming back to these six Bookmark Memories.

Each of these Bookmarks is designed to develop, not only the feelings of safety and connection, but "evidence" that "proves" you're safe, loved, and connected.

See if you can imagine each of the following memories as you read them. It may be difficult to do at first but if you find you aren't able to imagine them, notice what happens when you try. If any memories pop up that contradict these Bookmark Memories, change them, and practice the new ones.

It's possible that instead of memories, you just have a "knowing" or a feeling. If that's the case, ask yourself: ***How** do I know?* Or *Where in my childhood did I have that feeling?* Use the Detective Questions to find the memories, and then change them. Then, come back to the Bookmark Memories again. Use them as the "picture on the box of a jigsaw puzzle"— this is what you're aiming for.

It will take some time to get there, as you will need to first find the pieces and then put them together. When you get stuck, you can use the techniques in the following chapters to help you: (Generational Childhood Memory Transformation; The Due Justice Technique; Apology Letters; The Allowing Technique; Touchstones; Steppingstone Memories; Extra Detective Work; Anchor Memories; Answering Self-Talk; Rewriting Culture or Religion; and Reverse Engineering).

1. **Bedtime Story**

    You're a child, lying comfortably in bed. Your parents are sitting either side of you, reading you a bedtime story. They're smiling, taking it in turns to read, both of them fully engaged. You all laugh together as each parent does the funny voices of the characters.

    There's no need to know what the book or story is (although you can if that feels good). Focus in on the feeling of being together, and the relaxed, loving atmosphere.

    Feelings: *Safety, love, connection.*

2. **Light Up a Room**

    You're walking into a room, and your parents' faces light up as they see you. They immediately stop what they're doing, and fully focus on you. Again, you don't need details, just concentrate on the feeling as your parents' faces light up, and they stop what they're doing to focus on you because they love you so much.

    Feelings: *I'm important, valued, loved, worthy. I light up a room.*

3. **Empowerment to Speak**

   You're talking, and both of your parents are listening, allowing you to speak, nodding, understanding, and agreeing with you. You don't need to know what you're saying, or even the topic. You just need that feeling of talking, and them listening, engaged, and agreeing with you.

   Feelings: *I have the power to speak. It's safe to speak. I'm heard, I'm important, I'm interesting, I'm valuable, I'm safe.*

4. **The Power to Say No**

   You're saying "No" to your parents. You don't need to know what you're saying no to, just the feeling of saying "No" to something you don't want. Your parents say, kindly, compassionately, supportively, and lovingly: "Okay, of course, no problem. What would you like instead?"

   Feelings: *I have the power to say "No" and that is respected. I am empowered to choose what I want to experience. It's safe to say "No." Freedom.*

5. **It's Safe and Normal to Have Fun**

   You and both of your parents are playing a game or doing a fun activity together.

   Feelings: *I'm safe. It's safe to have fun. It's normal to feel good. Connection.*

6. **Physical Affection**

   You're sitting on the sofa with your parents either side of you, cuddling.

   Feelings: *Physical affection. I'm safe, loved, valuable, worthy. Peacefulness.*

Read through each of these Bookmark Memories and start with the one that's easiest for you to imagine. Focus on just that one to begin with, addressing and changing any negative memories that may contradict it. Then, once you're able to play that Bookmark Memory, feeling the good emotions with it, move on to the next easiest one. Keep going until you're able to read through each one, and imagine yourself and your parents in the scene, with the positive feelings.

RECAP:

- Bookmark Memories provide guidance for what you're aiming for, creating strong, specific data, including feelings of being safe and loved.
- When you can't imagine a Bookmark Memory with the positive feelings, use the techniques in the rest of this book to change any memories that contradict these Bookmarks, or address any resistance. Then come back to the Bookmark and try again.

If you find you can't imagine one or both of your parents being kind, compassionate, calm, or affectionate, you're not alone! And if you experience resistance to imagining them that way, Chapters 14 and 15 are your next stops!

Chapter 14

Generational Childhood Memory Transformation

"My father was an evil person. I spent my whole childhood in a state of fear, never knowing when he would beat me again just because he was angry about something that had nothing to do with me. I remember lying in bed at night, praying he'd been killed in a car accident on the way home. Dreading the sound of the key in the door, and the shouting that would precede him drunkenly staggering to my bedroom. I hate him. He was evil, and I can't imagine him being any other way."

—Janet.

One of the reasons it can be difficult to change some negative childhood memories is that we cannot imagine our parents differently. Think about the fact that our childhood experiences determine who we are and how the world works for us: If our parents had been raised differently, of course, they would have been different people, and therefore different parents. This is the reason we created Generational Childhood Memory Transformation.

We are all children in adult bodies, trying to navigate an adult world. It doesn't mean that what happened to you is excused, or okay in any way. It means that, although you had no power back then, you have the power now to give that little you the childhood they should have had!

Since the unconscious part of the brain can't tell the difference between reality and imagination, can't use logic or reason, and can't judge something as unrealistic, we can change our parents' and grandparents' childhoods in addition to our own. If your mother and father had been treated with love, kindness, and compassion throughout their childhoods, if they had felt safe, loved, respected, free, abundant, valued, encouraged, and supported, can you imagine the kind of parents they would have become? They would have treated you the same way they were treated.

How Generational Childhood Memory Transformation Works

Changing the childhoods of your parents and grandparents works on two levels:

1. It helps to answer your conscious resistance and objections.
2. It creates more and more networks in the brain that support what you want to achieve in your life, right now—proof that you come from a long line of _____ (whatever it is you want now).

How would you complete the following sentence?

"I come from a long line of people who _____."

Your aim, having changed generational childhoods, is to complete that sentence with whatever it is you want in your life, right now. For example, if you want to be healthy and energetic, you're aiming for: *"I come from a long line of people who are fit and healthy. My family all seem to have this amazing energy."* If you want to become a successful professional photographer, you're aiming for: *"I come from a long line of successful professional photographers."*

If you say your sentence to yourself, filling in the blank with whatever it is you want most in your life right now, and allowing yourself to pretend it's true for a moment, how does that feel? Don't worry about it not being true—the unconscious part of your brain doesn't know that. Remember being absorbed in a movie or TV show? Your brain and body behave as if what you're watching is real, and you feel the emotions that go with the story. Just for a moment, imagine the new statement is true, and notice how it feels to say you come from a long line of people who_____.

Imagine what would have happened if your grandparents and parents had grown up with whatever it is you want now. Again, remember that the unconscious part of your brain can't judge something as unrealistic, so, for example, you can create memories of your grandparents' parents trading stocks online, even though the internet may not have been invented back then. You can imagine your grandmother as a child, having a cell phone. You can imagine your grandfather as a child, riding to school in his father's Ferrari. Your subconscious won't question it. Any objections involving logic will be coming from your conscious mind—and you have control over that.

When thoughts of *"there weren't any cell phones back then,"* or any other logical arguments come up, be sure to answer those thoughts with, *"Yes, but the unconscious part of my brain doesn't know that."* Remind yourself that there aren't any dinosaurs, either, but you don't sit through *Jurassic Park* saying, *"But this isn't possible because dinosaurs don't exist. It would have been on the news."* Remind yourself of the movies and TV shows you've seen that are fiction, and unrealistic, and that you still allowed yourself to enjoy by suspending disbelief. That's what you're doing here. And you're doing it with the very specific and deliberate goal of changing your own brain chemistry and structure to create the changes you want to make in your life.

When to Use Generational Childhood Memory Transformation

Most people find they need this technique at some point as part of the process of changing negative childhood memories. Of course, there's no need to wait until you need it as it's a powerful and empowering technique to use anyway, but you'll know you need it when:

1. You're having trouble imagining a parent differently: *"I can't imagine my mother being affectionate,"* or *"I can't imagine my father being kind,"* for example.
2. You're struggling to imagine having what you want in your life, now.

A Word on Betrayal

If there is any suffering you know about in your family history, including cultural and religious suffering it's important to change that, too. You may find resistance to this because it can feel like you're denying or betraying those who suffered. Here's the answer to that:

Whatever happened back then is now over. It's not happening right now, except for neurons firing in a particular pattern in your brain.

Holding on to the suffering that happened doesn't help those who suffered, and it certainly doesn't help you and those around you today. But it does contribute to challenges you're experiencing in your life in ways you may be unaware of.

When you change those memories, you're changing the implicit memory, not the declarative memory. You will still be able to consciously know what happened, but it will no longer *define* you. It won't automatically determine the way you experience your life and interact with those around you.

Changing those memories of generational suffering to the opposite, positive, and empowering is like changing the GPS coordinates from where you are now, to where you want to get to. When you change your GPS from the city to the beach, you'll still remember that they were set to the city before. You're not denying those GPS coordinates were set to the city, you're not denying you're *currently* in the city. But you are *choosing* where you go *next*.

Feeling like you're betraying those who suffered or denying an important part of your heritage is a perspective created by existing childhood references that form the current structure of who you are and your worldview. And it's okay. Whether you change those memories or not is okay. It's just different results. If you have red ink in the printer, the pages you receive from that printer will be in red. If you want them in blue, you need to change the ink from red to blue. It's not about right or wrong. It's about cause and effect. What's in the printer is what comes out of the printer.

In the same way, what's in your memories is what you experience in your life. If you have a family legacy of suffering, of course it's going to determine who you are and how you experience the world. If you change those memories to the opposite, positive, and empowering, even though you'll consciously still remember what really happened, your self-image and worldview will automatically change, accordingly.

Contrary to what many of us were raised to believe, suffering is not beneficial and what doesn't kill you does *not* make you stronger.

There's a misperception that suffering and hardship contributes to strength. This couldn't be further from the truth. You have achieved what you've achieved *despite* the suffering, not because of it! Can you imagine what you'd have been able to achieve if you'd had everything you needed? Can you imagine what your family and ancestors would have achieved if they'd had everything they needed?

Think of it this way:

If you want to grow an apple tree, you don't kick the sapling around to make it stronger, right? You protect it, nurture it, and give it a chance to grow strong. Given that chance, it will automatically grow strong. If there are storms that damage it, and it grows anyway it's *despite* the damage from those storms, not because of it.

As children, the suffering and hardship we endure is certainly what makes us who we are—but not in a good way. Every child deserves to feel safe and loved. Every child deserves a childhood filled with love, safety, joy, fun, abundance, connection, respect, freedom, encouragement, and support. Every child deserves to feel heard, understood, and valued. Every child deserves to feel like they light up a room. Every child deserves to feel like they're the most important thing in their parents' lives. All these things result in a natural confidence, authentic kindness and compassion for others, and automatic success in life.

Suffering and hardship were the reality in the past, but they were the unnecessary "storms." Those who endured such experiences achieved what they achieved *despite* those experiences, not because of them.

If you had a magic wand and were able to travel back in time, wouldn't you give those generations of children in your family the most wonderful childhoods? Wouldn't you give them the gift of growing up safe, loved, happy, healthy, and financially abundant? You now have that opportunity. Because the unconscious part of your brain won't know the difference, you get to create what should have been. And the effects will be the power to create and experience those same feelings of being safe, loved, and happy, *now*.

In addition to the benefits for yourself, how will your new natural and automatic state full of positive emotions impact those around you? How will that new version of you affect those you love? Your own authentic peace, joy, and love will have countless positive effects on those you come into contact with without your even knowing about it. And what's more, you'll have more access to your cognitive thinking (prefrontal cortex), which will allow you to come up with solutions, notice opportunities, strategize, communicate, and process information in ways you've never been able to before.

You won't forget. You won't forget what happened. You're simply moving the disempowering memories from implicit (proving who you are and how the world works) to declarative (consciously remembering what happened, but no longer being defined by it). You now get to *decide* what those

GPS coordinates are—and thereby, what you get to experience in your life, moving forward.

What Does it Do?

We originally created this technique for the conscious mind, to answer the conscious objections: *"I can't imagine that person being like that,"* and *"My mother/father would never have done/said that."* The truth is, if they had been born to two loving parents who were happy, healthy, and couldn't wait to have their baby, and if they'd had a childhood filled with feelings of being loved, safe and valued, they would have grown into different people. Changing generational childhood memories enables you to overcome some of the conscious objections to changing your own childhood.

How to Use Generational Childhood Memory Transformation

You can either read through the meditation below or listen to the audio guide (or do both). You can find the link to download it in the Further Resources section of this book. As you do this:

1. Follow along until you experience resistance—contradicting or negative thoughts or feelings (for example: *"But her dad left before she was born"*). As soon as you notice one of these thoughts or a negative feeling, "press pause."
2. Change the contradicting childhood memories of that person, so that they're in alignment with this meditation.
3. Keep repeating steps one and two until you're able to read or listen to the full meditation without interruption from contradicting or negative thoughts or feelings.

Generational Childhood Meditation

Maternal Grandmother

Start by thinking of your mother's mother. Imagine she was born to two parents who were in-love, safe, financially stable, emotionally intelligent, affectionate, and confident, and couldn't wait to meet their baby girl.

Imagine that little girl growing up, feeling loved, secure, and supported. Imagine that when she started school, she was confident, made friends easily, and was able to concentrate in class. Everyone loved her.

Imagine the kind of teenager that little girl became. Since she was treated with kindness and compassion at home, that's how she automatically treated others.

She was top of her class and excelled at everything she did.

Now, imagine the kind of person she grew up to be.

Imagine the kind of wife and mother she was, having had that kind of childhood. She was confident, compassionate, respectful, loving, affectionate, successful, and joyful. She automatically treated her husband and child (your mother) in the same way she was treated.

Maternal Grandfather

Now, think about your mother's father. Imagine he was born to two parents who were in love, safe, financially stable, emotionally intelligent, affectionate, confident, and couldn't wait to meet their baby boy.

Imagine that little boy growing up, feeling loved, secure, and supported. Imagine that when he started school, he was confident, made friends easily, and was able to concentrate in class. Everyone loved him.

Imagine the kind of teenager that little boy became. Since he was treated with kindness and compassion at home, that's how he automatically treated others.

He was top of his class and excelled at everything he did.

Now, imagine the kind of person he grew up to be.

Imagine the kind of husband and father he was, having had that kind of childhood. He was confident, compassionate, respectful, loving, affectionate, successful, and joyful. He automatically treated his wife and child (your mother) in the same way he was treated.

Mother

Next, think about your mother. Imagine she was born to those two people. Those two people who grew up with so much love, kindness, compassion, abundance, affection, and security.

Imagine that little girl growing up, feeling loved, secure, and supported. Imagine that when she started school, she was confident, made friends easily, and was able to concentrate in class. Everyone loved her.

Imagine the kind of teenager that little girl became. Since she was treated with kindness and compassion at home, that's how she automatically treated others.

She was top of her class and excelled at everything she did.

Now, imagine the kind of person she grew up to be.

Imagine the kind of wife and mother she was while you were growing up. As a result of that childhood, she was confident, compassionate, respectful, loving, affectionate, successful, and joyful. She automatically treated her husband and child (you) in the same way she was treated.

Now, complete the exercise for your paternal grandmother, paternal grandfather, and father. Imagine the people they became.

Note:

- You can use this meditation for anyone you have trouble changing in your memories: teachers, siblings, and anyone else you wish were different.
- You can do this with entire cultures. Imagine if everyone in the

environment or country you grew up in had this kind of childhood—what would that culture be like?

RECAP:

- If your parents and grandparents had been raised with love, compassion, and kindness, and had felt safe, free, abundant, and
empowered during their childhood, they would have become different adults—and they would have automatically treated you the
way they were treated.
- Generational Childhood Memory Transformation is a gift to the
child in you, allowing you to change your own negative childhood
memories to the opposite, positive, and empowering.

Remind yourself that this is not about denying anything, this is about
choosing the GPS coordinates to match what you want to experience in
your life, now and moving forward.

Brain Plunger: The Due Justice Technique

"Shields up, red alert!"
—James T. Kirk (*Star Trek*)

You may find, like many people, that when you try to use the Generational Childhood Memory Transformation technique from Chapter 14 that there is no way you're able to get past the resistance. That resistance is the brain's version of the deflector shields in *Star Trek*!

The Due Justice Technique is a powerful unblocker for clearing the resistance to changing negative childhood memories and it can make all the difference to your results. Think of this technique as a drain plunger (or brain plunger!). When you feel stuck, your "sink" may be blocked, and you can use this "plunger" to clear it.

When to Use the Due Justice Technique

There are two main reasons for using the Due Justice Technique:

1. When you feel resistant to changing certain memories, or memories of certain people.
2. When you feel there's something bothering you, but you can't identify what it might be from your childhood.

What Does it Do?

We've found that most people (including ourselves) have some resistance to changing certain negative childhood memories, whether it's regarding one or both parents, someone else, or the memories of specific events. However that resistance may be experienced, the reason for the resistance is that changing that memory is perceived by the brain as dangerous.

Since our top unconscious priority is survival, one of our survival mechanisms is to keep our focus on any perceived "danger." If you take your eyes off the "bear" you could die. Changing a negative childhood memory can feel the same as ignoring danger.

Why it's Difficult to Let Go of Anger

Holding on to anger is not stubbornness, or even a conscious decision—it's protection mode. Anger is the "fight" of the fight-flight-freeze emergency state—it's the equivalent of having your fists up in a fight or having your deflector shields up in *Star Trek*.

As long as the security system detects a threat, it's not going to let down those shields! And the conscious mind often cannot override that security system by decision alone. The security system needs to be reprogrammed. But when the threat seems particularly lethal (based on past experience) that security system may not allow you anywhere near it since the danger is so intense.

The Due Justice Technique helps that part of you to "annihilate" the threat, which then allows you to go in and reprogram the security system.

In other words, once you've used the Due Justice Technique, you will then be able to go ahead and change the negative childhood memories, since the "threat" has been removed.

How the Due Justice Technique Works

The Due Justice Technique works with the subconscious mind and the "child" in you to ensure that the "justice due" is carried out, and closure is achieved. That little child in you finally has someone to stand up for them, justice has been done, and you have the closure that that part of you needs so you can move forward in letting go and making changes.

Since the unconscious part of the brain can't tell the difference between reality and imagination, as far as that part of your brain is concerned, this activity is *real*. Justice really has been done. Closure really has been achieved. This is *why* the Due Justice Technique works.

How to Use the Due Justice Technique

Set aside around two hours when you won't be disturbed. It's worth doing whatever it takes to prioritize doing the Due Justice Technique, since it will affect everything else in your life. Choose a time when you'll be able to sleep after you've completed the exercise, so, a couple of hours before bedtime or on a day off, for example, is ideal. According to brain research, the brain processes and organizes information from experiences during sleep[59].

1. Find yourself a notepad and pen. (We've found that this technique works better when it's handwritten, rather than typed).
2. Write a letter you'll never send. Note: Many therapy modalities use an unsent letter technique for processing emotions and gaining clarity—The Due Justice Technique is different! We discuss the main differences in the section below.

   Start with the person from your childhood who you feel harmed you the most. And then write to everyone who raised you.

   Remember: It doesn't matter whether you consciously understand or not, and whether you've consciously forgiven the person or not—the unconscious part of your brain, and that little child in you, cannot use logic or reason and cannot understand. That

---

59   Andrea Ballesio & Nicola Cellini. "Updating Internal Cognitive Models during Sleep." Journal of Neuroscience. 39(11), 2019:1966–68. doi: https://doi.org/10.1523/JNEUROSCI.2926-18.2019

part of your brain just experiences the world and then interprets the experience to mean something about who you are and how the world works.

In this letter, make sure you get everything out of you and onto the page. Swear, be unreasonable, use ALL CAPs and lots of exclamation marks! Really let them have it! No one's ever going to see this letter, so you can say everything that's inside you.

Although you're not going to send the letter, the unconscious part of your brain (and that child in you) will believe that the recipient has received it—that justice has been done—and that you have closure.

This will free you to move forward, whereas before you've been stuck.

3. Read the letter through, imagining the other person reading it, or imagine hearing that part of you speaking it to them.
4. Once you feel you're finished with it, tear it up and throw it away, or burn it ceremoniously.
5. Sleep! You'll feel drained and you'll need to sleep. Your brain will need to process the experience and information. You need to sleep in order to get the full benefit of the exercise.

An example from Steve:

I have had three distinctive experiences regarding sleep and writing Due Justice letters. After I wrote the first letter, I remember feeling a surprising sense of release, and quite drained, as a result of engaging in the process of writing for nearly two hours. I had been so wrapped up in the writing that I actually had no idea how much time had passed. I went to bed shortly after completing the letter. I remember waking several times during the night with disturbing dreams. In the morning, I recounted the experience to Odille, who reminded me: "Yes, your brain must have had a lot to process."

The second occurrence was after writing yet another significant Due Justice letter in which I felt the release of much early childhood sadness. However, the sleep I experienced that night, after writing this letter, was perhaps the most peaceful that I can ever remember. I awoke the next morning in such a deliciously calm and beautiful state that I stayed in bed soaking in every moment of the feeling.

A short time later, I wrote a third Due Justice letter, and I admit that I was secretly hoping for another wonderful night's sleep. However, after this third letter, I had what I would describe as a "regular" night's sleep.

In speaking with my clients about their experiences of the Due Justice Technique, several have reported similar experiences with how they sleep afterward. The reason I share these examples here is to highlight the possibility that you may experience some differences in your pattern of sleep following the writing of a Due Justice letter, and to say that this is expected and quite natural as your brain is going through its usual function of processing data as you sleep.

Due Justice Technique vs Other Unsent Letter Techniques

The reason the Due Justice Technique works is this: The unconscious part of the brain doesn't know the difference between reality and imagination and will believe that the guilty party has been told off, and that justice has been done. This releases the need to continue to hold on to the past and frees you to move forward. The "danger" has been "annihilated," and you are now safe to change those memories.

Key Differences Between an Unsent Letter and the Due Justice Technique

Many different therapy processes use an unsent letter to help process emotions; gain understanding and objectivity; release emotions; make amends; and gain clarity. However, the Due Justice Technique is not about understanding or objectivity. The aim of it is to:

- allow the unconscious part of the brain (and the hurt child inside you) to feel that justice has been done
- give the unconscious part of the brain (and that inner child) a feeling that someone finally stood up for you and that the "danger" is now gone
- give the unconscious part of the brain (and the child inside) closure and a feeling of being safe

You may find that you need to write more than one letter. It varies from person to person. The end goal is to rewrite your childhood, so the number of Due Justice letters you need to write will depend on whether you're able to imagine your parents and others differently or not. If you feel stuck at any point, or you're not getting the results you want, write another Due Justice letter.

Resistance to the Due Justice Technique

It's important to realize that you will probably resist writing these letters. That's completely natural. Do it despite the resistance. When something is going to lead to massive changes, we naturally and automatically experience unconscious resistance. It's part of the survival mechanism that keeps us safe by keeping us the same.

You may think you have perfectly logical reasons for not writing these letters, but here's what's happening behind the scenes:

The unconscious part of your brain is referring to the fact that this would completely change the status quo, which means you will no longer be in alignment with your "tribe," or the way things have always been. It sees this as a threat to your survival. Remember, this unconscious part of your brain can't use logic or reason the way your conscious mind can. So, the fact that you consciously really want more money, or a happy relationship, better health, more freedom, or success, doesn't matter. Your brain is programmed to keep you the same as you are now, since staying the same equals survival. You may not be happy, or you may be in pain, but you're still alive.

Since the brain's main driver is survival, as we start to make any core changes it triggers the production of stress chemicals, which create feelings, sensations, emotions, and impulses that will deter us from moving forward on this path of core change.

As you become consciously aware of these (often very subtle) sensations, impulses, emotions, and feelings, you automatically interpret them to mean something "logical." A logical reason for not taking the step of writing this letter.

For example: *I'm too tired; I'll do it later; I don't have time; I've done this before; I have to do X first; I've forgiven them; this is silly; I have nothing to say; I don't need to do this; I'm scared; I don't have any negative feelings; I love them, I don't want to say bad things about them.*

This is how the unconscious survival part of your brain controls your conscious mind and it does so in order to keep you "safe" by keeping you the same.

When you feel resistant to doing the Due Justice Technique, regardless of the "logical reasons" recognize that resistance as your brain trying to keep you the same, and then do it anyway!

If you're unable to change your negative childhood memories, the Due Justice Technique, used as directed, will clear whatever's blocking you.

An example from Steve:

Encountering resistance to writing a Due Justice letter is something that I understand firsthand. I was working on changing some childhood memories regarding my father, and creating new memories and new stories with him, but these new memories didn't connect. They didn't feel real. I could cognitively recite these new memories in my mind, but in the background, I kept hearing the voice that said, "Well, that would have never happened!"

At this point, Odille and I were teaching our clients about the Due Justice Technique. Whenever a client was having difficulty in changing a memory, I advised them to use the Due Justice Technique because I knew it would make the difference. However, I was encountering a rather subtle form of resistance to using the technique myself. It didn't feel very strong—I just knew that I did not need to write a Due Justice letter. I was certain that I wasn't harboring anything negative about my father. I had gone through traditional training as a psychotherapist and had engaged in activities that had us writing letters to our parents that we wouldn't send. I had dealt with all of this, I was over all of that, I had moved on.

I remember discussing my dilemma of not being able to change the memories of my childhood with my father with Odille, and she very kindly and wisely advised me to write a Due Justice letter to him. I remember feeling a little disappointed, and certain that I was just missing something else because I had no negative feelings for my dad.

After about three months of procrastinating, and finding other things to be doing, I finally leaned into the activity of writing the Due Justice letter to my father. I remember mixing up a nice, iced beverage and sitting down with a new legal pad and my favorite pen—this wouldn't take long.

Fourteen pages and two hours later, I emerged, and conceded to Odille, "Well...I guess there was some stuff there." I had a long childhood pattern of repressing or "swallowing" emotions, so it wasn't too surprising to realize that there may have been some hidden emotions.

The following day, I returned to the new memories of my father that had been problematic before and I was able to feel them as real! Nearly all my one-to-one clients have experienced some resistance to writing the Due Justice letters, but once they've done them, they've always experienced release and insight, and have been able to move forward with creating the empowering new childhood memories that lead to transformational change.

Frequently Asked Questions About the Due Justice Technique

Can I write the Due Justice letter to my boss/spouse/ex/work colleague?

Absolutely, but you'll need to write it to those who raised you first. Remember that everything you're experiencing now—including relationships with your boss, spouse, ex, and others—is based on your childhood experiences. As you encounter the challenges with those in your life today, the unconscious part of your brain refers to the "evidence" (in the form of implicit childhood memories) that "proves" who you are, how the world works, and what certain experiences mean. It then prompts your brain and body to produce chemicals. Those chemicals create sensations that your conscious mind interprets as emotions. Write the letter to those who raised you first and change the childhood memories of those people. Then, when you move forward to the people in your life today, the changes will be quicker and more effective.

Who should I write to first?

Start with the person for whom you feel the strongest negative emotions. If you have issues with someone in your life right now (boss/ex/spouse/neighbor), ask yourself who they remind you of from your childhood. Then, write a Due Justice letter to that person first.

Do I have to write? Can't I just imagine saying it to the person, in my mind?

The act of writing the letter creates the effect. You may have experienced the feeling of having a lot to do and trying to keep the information in your mind. When you make a to-do list, it frees that part of your brain, and you can think more clearly. Another example is: If you can't sleep because your mind is too active, have a notepad and pen next to your bed, and "unpack" your head by writing down what it is you're thinking about. You'll then find it easier to go to sleep. The purpose of writing the letter is to get all of that "stuff" out of you, and onto the page.

Do I have to write for two hours?

No. The two-hour time slot is just a guide. It may take you longer to get everything out, or it may take far less time. Just write until you feel you've expressed everything you need to.

I can't think of anything to say/ I don't know how to start.

Just start with: "Dear _____" and then write whatever comes to your mind—even if it's something like *"How are you? I am fine. It's sunny here today, and I'm having spaghetti for supper..."* Just start writing anything, and you'll find that the emotions start to come automatically. Before you know it, you'll be expressing your deepest feelings. Keep reminding yourself that no one's ever going to see this letter, so you can really let rip. The goal is to get everything out of you and in black and white on the page.

Does it make a difference if I write by hand or type?

Yes. If you are unable to write by hand, then typing will be better than not doing it at all. But do prioritize writing it by hand if you can.

I can't feel any anger and my letter is understanding and polite.

Try these options:

- Take a moment to imagine that these things happened to another child. If you have children, or you know children, imagine the people who raised you treated those children the way they treated you.

- Remind yourself that no one will ever read this letter, and that the purpose of it is to "clean out the infected wound," and then you will destroy it.
- Take a break and then try changing childhood memories of that person. Notice what happens inside you when you try to change those memories. Then come back and try writing the letter again.
- Remind yourself that the purpose of this letter is not to understand or excuse the person you're writing to—it is to give voice to the little you and let go of the emotions.

As I read through the letter, I can imagine them arguing with me, justifying, excusing, and defending their actions.

Notice what they're saying, and then add your responses to your letter (or write another letter in response). Even if you just reply with, "Bullsh*t! You don't know what you're talking about! **** off!!" Keep answering any responses you imagine from them, until there are none left, and you're able to feel closure. Also remind yourself that it's not actually them arguing—they're not here, and they can't fit inside your head. Those arguments and justifications are just the result of neural networks in your own brain, firing in a certain sequence, based on your previous experiences of that person. And you get to change that sequence now. You get to take control and fire your own neurons in a way that will empower and benefit you. You may also find the technique in Chapter 16 on Apology Letters helpful.

I feel guilty about saying negative things about this person.

Remind yourself that they're not going to see it and that whatever you write is already inside you. That's the key here. This is not about creating bad thoughts and feelings, this is about getting what you're already carrying inside you—which is affecting you—out, and letting it go. So, rather than a reason for guilt, it's a reason for freedom. This process will rid you of the negative emotions so that you can have more love, affection, appreciation, joy, fun, abundance, and connection in your life and in your relationships with others.

Can I end the letter with something positive—appreciation, forgiveness, or love, for example?

If you include any positivity—reasoning, understanding, seeing it from their point of view, or anything else positive (even right at the end)—it's like telling a child who has been badly beaten that you are going to deliver justice to those who assaulted her, and so she watches you deliver that punishment…and then she watches as you appease her attackers, try to see things from their point of view, thank them, and tell them you love them. Remember, the child in you and that unconscious part of your brain cannot use reason or logic. So, any positive message will feel like a betrayal. Self-betrayal. Let this letter stand alone—purely Due Justice—with no filters, no reasoning, no understanding, no seeing from someone else's point of view. Then, after you've read it, destroyed it, and slept, if you still want to you can write a letter of understanding, appreciation, and forgiveness. A separate letter. Only then can you move forward with positivity, love, and appreciation, which will then be more genuine, more natural, more free, and more effective. And what better way to forgive and move forward than changing those childhood memories to the opposite, positive, and empowering!

I wrote the letters, but I don't feel anything different.

That's okay. Not everyone experiences a noticeable emotional shift at the time. Just go ahead and create that new childhood, now. If you have memories come up that contradict the new childhood, change them. If you find you're still experiencing resistance to changing memories or creating that new empowering childhood, you may need to write another Due Justice letter. There is no right or wrong—the letter is only a "plunger" to "unblock the drain" so that you can continue washing your dishes. In other words, a way of clearing any unconscious anger, hurt, and resentment that may be preventing you from letting go of the past and moving forward by changing the childhood memories to more empowering references for your life, now.

RECAP:

- The purpose of the Due Justice Technique is to lower resistance to changing negative childhood memories.

- It's important to get everything that's inside you out and onto the page—with no apologies, no reasoning, no understanding or forgiveness, no positive spin. This is about the child in you feeling like someone finally stood up for them, and justice has been done.
- After you've written the letter, sleep will help your brain to process the changes.
- Once you've slept, go back to changing the negative childhood memories. If you still can't change them, you may need to write more Due Justice letters.

Shields Still Up?

If you find you haven't been able to get closure from the Due Justice Technique, you may need the Apology Letters in the next chapter.

Chapter 16

I Can't Hear You! Apology Letters

The idea of Apology Letters was created by one of our wonderful clients, a member of our Daily Group community, Ilja Vanoppen. Ilja found that, for her, writing the Due Justice letters was only a part of it. Following them with an Apology Letter—addressed to that little her—as a reply from each parent (and anyone else she used the Due Justice Technique for) made a more powerful difference to her being able to move forward with changing childhood memories.

Here's the Apology Letter Technique, in Ilja's own words:

Have you ever felt (while doing or after writing a Due Justice letter) as if:

- *You can keep on writing and writing Due Justice letters?*

- *You are talking to a wall while writing a Due Justice letter, or just in general?*

- *You really needed to be acknowledged in your (emotional) pain?*

- *You are still waiting on the apologies that were so needed, but you never received?*

If so, then an "Apology letter" might be what you need.

Here are some guidelines to get you started. Always incorporate whatever YOU need to hear in your apology letters.

1. *Start by letting that person address you in a loving way (e.g. "My Dear...")*

2. *Have that person **acknowledge** whatever you have said in your Due Justice letter. You can incorporate words like, "You are absolutely right! Every word you said, you are right! And I deserved to hear those words."*

3. *Use words that you need to hear, like: "I hear you, I understand you, you are right, we are listening now, I am proud of you for speaking up and telling me/us," etc.*

4. *This way you KNOW your message has been received (so you're no longer talking to a wall!) and that you have been understood.*

5. *Have that person **acknowledge** that what they did/said to you was wrong/hurtful/traumatic. Let them take responsibility and ownership for their actions.*

6. *Have that person **apologize** to you. This can either be a general apology, or you can make it as explicit as you want/need.*

7. *Have this person say something like, "It was never your job to take care of me, in whatever way or form,*

psychologically and/or emotionally. I hereby take back all the responsibilities that I have ever put on you. Responsibilities that were my job."

8. Continue with, *"And I give you back the freedom to just be you. The freedom to be your loving, creative, carefree, brave, wonderful, magical, healthy, most intelligent you. Because that is what you deserve, and you should have had it in the first place!"*

9. You can end your Apology Letter in whatever way you want:

    a. With some loving words

    b. By summing up more specifically everything that you needed and deserved in your childhood

    c. With a question: *"If it is okay with you, can I make it up to you and give you everything that you deserved and needed?"* You can then decide how you want to answer.

       It looks as though you're giving them permission, but in fact you are granting yourself permission to give yourself the gift of new experiences, of a new childhood!

—*Ilja Vanoppen*

When to Use Apology Letters

If you've written a Due Justice letter, and you find you're still experiencing resistance to changing your childhood memories with a particular person, using the Apology Letter Technique will help to give that child inside you the acknowledgement and reassurance they deserve, helping that part of you to feel safe to move forward.

RECAP:

- The Apology Letters are letters you imagine being written to you, by those who wronged you.
- Include in them everything you need to hear from that person—acknowledgement, apology, reassurance, amends, affection, remorse, and anything else you need.
- Remind yourself that this is all about you—you get to choose what's included in the letters, whether or not you think that person would actually say those things in reality.

Stuck in Negative Emotions?

Sometimes, despite all efforts, you'll find your vehicle stuck in the mud. You may not be able to move forward at that time, but there is something you can do that will help to get you unstuck.

Chapter 17

Stuck in the Mud: The Allowing Technique

An example from Steve:

I had recently begun working with Barry, who was dealing with anxiety and depression and seemed to be perpetually in a triggered state. As we engaged in the usual detective work of looking for foundational memories, Barry found that he was struggling to find any memories.

During the session he was clearly experiencing a deep emotional trigger, however, nothing was coming to mind, and I could sense his frustration as he confessed that he just didn't have many memories from childhood. Instead of pushing it, I suggested that we just stop and be with whatever was going on in the moment.

I realized later that I had been inspired to tap into my 15-year mindfulness meditation practice. I asked Barry to imagine "taking a step back" to see if he could identify the physical sensations of the emotions that he was experiencing. It was a tightness in his chest and a queasy, nauseous feeling in the pit of his stomach. Again, I asked him to be in the space of taking a step back and asked him to just be with or observe those sensations. Did they have any other characteristics? Did they have a color or a texture? Did they have a size or expression?

Barry allowed himself to simply be with what was coming as a result of quietly observing. He said that he was seeing an angry dark "blob" wrapped in chains at the bottom of a deep hole. I encouraged Barry to stay in observer mode, as he allowed the "blob" to just be there. I asked if there was anything he could do for it, to help it feel a little better in the moment. Barry said, "I think it needs a hug." I asked Barry to create that hug: "Imagine wrapping your arms around that blob... How does that feel? Imagine what it feels like for the blob. Does the blob need to say anything?"

Behind the Scenes of the Allowing Technique

The Allowing Technique is designed to bring down the level of stress chemicals when the other tools aren't working. It's about becoming the "observer" and adjusting your perception and focus to slow the production of those stress chemicals.

As we know, negative emotions can become a vicious circle of stress chemicals and negative thoughts—each perpetuating and fueling the other. If you're able to use Zero Tolerance, that's the quickest, most effective way to break that circle. However, it's not always possible, especially at the beginning of this journey before you've fully developed the skill of controlling your chemical state. So, when you find that you're triggered, and unable to change your focus, you can use the Allowing Technique to start turning off that stress chemicals "tap."

Bearing in mind that thoughts are connections between neurons that trigger matching chemicals, the action of bringing your thoughts in to focus just on the physical sensations and firing those neurons in the pattern of: *"It's okay to feel this right now. It's okay. It's just a physical sensation,"* helps to interrupt the conscious mind's automatic activity of looking for reasons for the negative feelings. You're choosing which neurons to fire and in which pattern and that results in a switch in chemicals, which in turn will start to reduce the intensity of the negative emotions.

Back to Barry

We took a step back and noticed what was happening in the scene. Barry reported that the blob was now beginning to morph into an image of himself about five years old, in his darkened bedroom. I asked Barry to stay in "observer mode" and notice: What is that little you experiencing? How does he feel about your presence in the room? What do you feel he needs? "Not to be alone, and not to be stuck in the room," Barry replied. "Great," I encouraged. "Now imagine giving him a hug and creating a way for him to get out of the room." Barry hesitated, and then said that "little Barry" didn't want to go out the door, because "that's where they are."

I suggested that he use his imagination and help little Barry create a way out of the room. Barry imagined a fun secret passageway out of his second-story bedroom that led to a door to the backyard of the house. Again, we stepped back from the scene and noticed what was happening. I asked him to describe the feelings in his chest and stomach. "I feel like I can begin to breathe…it feels lighter," he replied.

Through this process of just being with the sensations, Barry was later able to connect with long-buried childhood feelings and could empower "little Barry" to leave the bedroom, and no longer feel alone. He was able to unearth and change the foundational memories of abusive parents and a chaotic environment.

What the process with Barry enabled us to see is that many of us often end up "struggling" with negative feelings and emotions. We don't like them, and we don't want to be feeling them, and we have come up with ways to fight them, or deny them, or pretend that they are not there. The truth is that the feelings and emotions are part of us, and whenever we are engaged in the "struggle" we are someplace on the "fight-flight-freeze" stress response scale.

Barry's experience showcases how taking a step back and getting into "observer mode" puts us in a more empowered place. Practicing the Allowing Technique not only begins to shift the neurochemical state; it also has the potential to provide insight into foundational memories that need to be transformed.

When to Use the Allowing Technique

When you find yourself emotionally triggered, the first step is to recognize that what you're feeling (as real as it feels) is the effect of stress chemicals in your system. The second step is to answer any negative thoughts using logic, and then do whatever you can to bring down the level of those stress chemicals, and that means changing your focus. Use one of the suggestions in Part Three of this book, or one of your own ideas. Do whatever it takes to change your focus to turn off the "stress chemicals tap" and turn on the "feel-good chemicals tap."

When you find the emotions are too intense, and you can't change your focus, or the feelings are not reducing, try using the Allowing Technique.

What Does it Do?

The way our survival system works means that it can be very difficult to take our focus off the bad stuff once we're triggered because the effects of stress chemicals keep our attention on the "danger." As we judge those negative feelings and try to stop them, we can pump more stress chemicals into our system—heightening that state of emergency.

Think of this as arm-wrestling. While you're arm-wrestling with the feeling, you're holding it in your experience and adding more and more struggle and stress. In order to release the feeling, you need to start by letting go of its hand! The Allowing Technique helps you to do this.

As Steve says: *"When the house is on fire, the priority is to get out of the house. Once you're outside of the house, and the fire is out, then you can go back in and find out what caused the fire."* In other words, when you're very triggered, that is not the time to look for the cause of that trigger. Because every thought that explores the possible causes and reasons for that trigger only results in pumping more stress chemicals into your system.

The Allowing Technique allows you to bring those stress chemicals down enough, to allow you to, at a later time, find and change the childhood memories that are providing the foundation for that trigger in the first place.

Note:

Like all of these "Rest and Repair Stops," the Allowing Technique is not a destination. It's not a stand-alone technique. It's a pitstop to get you back on the road—another tool to clear the way, to get you to the end destination of a new childhood. A new childhood is what will automatically result in the changes you want to experience in your life.

How to Use the Allowing Technique

You can practice this right now so that you're more familiar with it when you really need it.

1. Whatever you're feeling—emotional or physical—start to notice the physical sensations of that feeling. Notice where in your body you feel it, and home in on what that physical sensation is.
2. Now, tell yourself that it's okay to feel this sensation, that it doesn't mean anything, it's just a sensation, and allow yourself to experience it. Repeat this to yourself, as you would to a child who was feeling frightened. *"It's okay, it's just a sensation, it doesn't mean anything. It's okay to feel it. It's okay for it to be here."*

3. As you do this, do you notice any changes in the sensation? Is it the same? Is it more, or less? Does it move?

4. Once you feel the intensity come down, you can try moving your focus to your chosen favorite color or one of the other suggestions in Part Three of this book.

The Allowing Technique Extended Version:

If you follow Steps 1 to 3, and you find the intensity doesn't shift, or that you still aren't able to move forward with changing your focus, use this extended version of The Allowing Technique:

5. As you're noticing the physical sensation of what you're feeling, imagine stepping back from that sensation so that it's in front of you, and seeing it as an entity—separate from you. What does it look like? If you don't have a visual, just notice how you know what it looks like (or how you are experiencing it).

6. Now, ask that "entity" what it needs so it can feel a little better right now. Notice the first thing that pops into your mind. And see if you can imagine giving whatever that is to this entity.

7. Ask the entity if it has anything to say.

8. Perhaps ask that entity where it would like to live, or where it might feel safe. Or you can ask yourself where you *think* that entity would like to live. Then, *allow* it to go and live there.

9. Whenever you think of that feeling again, remind yourself that it's no longer here, it's living in the place you allowed it to go and live in.

Think of the Allowing Technique as a way to get your car out of the mud. Imagine your car is stuck in the mud, and the more you try to move forward by pressing the accelerator, the more the wheels spin, and the further and further your car becomes entrenched.

To get your car out of the mud, you need to take your foot off the accelerator and, in the first instance, allow your car to be in the mud.

Allowing it to be there means you're not spinning those wheels and digging it in deeper. It's okay for your car to be in the mud for the moment. You're safe, there's nothing dangerous right now, it's just mud.

Then, when you're ready, and you're certain your car is not sinking deeper, you can get out of the car, call AAA, push it, or whatever other options you have, without spinning those wheels again.

In this analogy, pressing the accelerator while the car is stuck in the mud is the equivalent of struggling with the negative emotions when you're stuck in a negative emotional state. Taking your foot off the accelerator and allowing your car to be in the mud for the moment while you come up with a plan is the equivalent of doing the Allowing Technique.

Calling AAA or pushing your car out of the mud once the wheels have stopped spinning is the equivalent of then using one of the Zero Tolerance Techniques (from Chapter 11) to change your chemical state, once the Allowing Technique has brought the stress chemicals down enough to be able to move forward with another technique.

RECAP:

- The Allowing Technique is for those times when you're unable to change your focus and lower the stress chemicals using the other techniques, or for when you just don't know what you're feeling or what's bothering you.
- The purpose of the Allowing Technique is to bring down the stress chemicals by ceasing to struggle with the negative feelings. You're allowing the sensations to just be there and reassuring yourself that it's okay to feel those sensations.
- Once the stress chemicals have reduced, be sure to change your focus, and play new childhood memories.

And when it all seems too much...

Are We There Yet?
Touchstones

When you feel you have too many thoughts that interfere with your end result, and your mind keeps focusing on the challenges and hurdles, and especially when you can't see how you'll achieve the results you want—use a Touchstone.

Touchstones are a moment in time that you can "touch" frequently throughout your day, and particularly when you're triggered. Touchstones have no details, they're just one moment with a strong positive feeling. An example of a Touchstone is imagining you've achieved your goal, and you're exclaiming excitedly: *"Yes! I did it!"* Just that moment. No details of how it worked out, or what happened. Just that end moment that represents it worked out perfectly.

When Do You Need a Touchstone?

A Touchstone is designed to simplify your focus and keep you "facing" the right way. We are always moving forward in the direction in which we're facing, so you need to keep yourself "facing" the destination you want to end up in. A Touchstone helps you to do this more easily.

Imagine you're driving on the road from the city to the countryside, and your focus is the direction your car is pointing in the moment. While you're thinking of the countryside, you're heading toward it. Each time you think about the fact that you're not there yet, you veer off the road. Each time you think about the city, you start heading back there. Your attention and focus are your steering. But, of course, it can be very difficult to keep your focus on the countryside when you're surrounded by storms and detours and scary scenery. Practicing Zero Tolerance and using a Touchstone will make it easier for you to stay on the road.

How to Use a Touchstone

The key to the power of a Touchstone is that there are no details. It's just one moment in time, with feeling, that represents the outcome.

1. Take a deep breath, close your eyes, and imagine you've been able to wave a magic wand and achieved the results you want. Allow yourself to feel the good feelings and notice how it feels and where in your body you feel them.

2. Now, think about expressing that feeling in a moment in time. It could be saying to yourself, *"Yes! I did it!"* or a moment of high-fiving a friend, saying, *"YES!!"* It could be a moment of gratitude, saying, *"Thank you, thank you, thank you!"* or a moment of peace, appreciating the results with, *"Thank you so much!"* It could be a moment of wonder saying, *"That's amazing!"* Choose a short phrase that comes with a strong, positive feeling that represents the end result.

3. Repeat that moment in time, over and over, in your mind and really focus on the feeling. No details, no how, where, when, who—just that one moment that represents success, with the feeling that goes with it.

4. Now, use that as your Touchstone by "touching" it frequently. Play it first thing in the morning, as soon as you're awake, last thing at night, as you go to sleep, and many times during the day. Do it even when you don't feel like doing it! As you can see, it takes hardly any time at all, and it will help to keep you on track toward the destination you want to end up in. It will help you to spend less time "off road."

An example from Odille:

Toward the end of 2016, I was living in Gloucester, England. A lot had changed inside me, and although my finances had improved, I still wasn't where I wanted to be. In addition to this, the three visits to America that year had reinforced how much I wanted to live there. I had lived in the USA when I was much younger, traveling with family from when I was 19 to 21 years old, and I really loved the feeling of being there.

I thought the only way I would be able to move to America would be through accumulating a lot of money and starting a successful business, and then investing in property or business there. My focus was on building my coaching business to hopefully increase my income enough to be able to invest. I knew it would take many years, but it was the only route I could see at that time.

As I walked around the neighborhood, a lot of doubts cropped up. Gloucester is a lovely place, and if I hadn't wanted to live in America so badly, I'd have been happy staying there. It was definitely my second choice. But the pull to live in the States was so strong, it was almost an ache.

So, I invented the Touchstone. Instead of pondering the details and hows and whether I would evers…I created one moment in time that had the feeling of already being there. My Touchstone was, "I LOVE my life!" At first, saying that phrase, while surrounded by reality didn't bring up much more than objections. "I'm 52 years old, with no way I can see to live where I really want to live."

I answered these thoughts by reminding myself that we can't "see around corners" and I had no idea what the road ahead would hold. But I did know that I am always moving forward in the direction I'm facing, so, as long as I was able to keep redirecting (correcting that steering) to "I LOVE my life," it didn't matter what route I took, I would end up with that feeling. It didn't matter whether I actually did end up living in America, or somewhere else. It didn't matter what the details were—I would still end up at that destination of "I LOVE my life!"

We think we know what will make us happy, what will make us feel safe, and what will bring us peace, but the truth is, the only place we experience those feelings is inside ourselves. That's been said by a lot of people in different ways, but consider this: The way we feel is literally created by chemicals inside our own brains and bodies. Nothing outside of us (not even the environment in which we live or work) can create those chemicals. They are created inside us. Of course, they are created in response to things that are outside of us, but that response is determined by just two things (both are controllable, with practice).

1. *Implicit memories from childhood*
2. *Wherever we're putting our focus in the moment*

So, as I changed my negative childhood memories and practiced the new ones, I also started repeating that Touchstone: "I LOVE my life," even as I looked at "reality" around me. Even as I experienced challenges and disappointments: "I LOVE my life." At first, I was faking it. I didn't feel the feeling of loving my life, but I said it anyway. Over and over. In addition to practicing my new childhood memories and making sure that feeling of "I LOVE my life" was in those new memories. And the more I repeated that phrase—first thing in the morning, as soon as I was awake, many times throughout the day, and last thing at night as I was falling asleep—the easier and stronger the feeling became.

I remember walking through the neighborhood, saying to myself, out loud: "I LOVE my life," with the feeling. I remember walking through the streets, listening to the song on my phone: Love My Life by Robbie

Williams, over and over. I remember using "I LOVE my life," as a guide rail in the dark when I was emotionally triggered.

I had no intention of getting married again. I wasn't even interested in a relationship. My entire focus was on building my business and sharing what I'd learned about childhood memories with others who were struggling. "I LOVE my life," whatever that would be. I kept repeating just that moment. No details, no hows or wheres.

When I boarded the flight to Los Angeles in February 2017, I was excited to be returning to the USA, and looking forward to the seminar I was attending in Oklahoma City later that month. I had no idea that this was going to be the corner around which I couldn't see until I got around it. The turn in the road that I wouldn't see coming that would lead me to that end result of "I LOVE my life!" in a way I could never have imagined.

Still focused on learning as much as I could, and building my business, I arrived at the seminar on the Friday, ready for the week-long event to start on the Saturday. I was sharing a hotel suite with two friends and enjoying catching up with many more who were also attending. I was happy, and loving meeting new people as well. A far cry from the previous reclusive me, a couple of years before—another shift created from changing those childhood memories.

On the Saturday, Steve introduced himself to me. By Monday, I knew this was the person I was going to spend the rest of my life with. We hadn't got to know each other much at all, and he had no idea that I was smitten, but I knew. It was so unusual for me to have that "knowing," but it was as if I'd traveled fast-forward in time to where I am now, and then, popped back again, with what I know and feel now—that Steve is the love of my life. I'd had no idea that someone like him even existed, that a relationship like this was even possible—for anyone, never mind me. "I LOVE my life!" I continued with that phrase—it was now on automatic.

Fast forward to August 2017, and I am living in America, married to the love of my life, an outcome I could never have seen coming. And I genuinely LOVE my life. Every morning when I wake up, every evening when I go to sleep, and frequently throughout my days, and the adventures Steve and I have had together so far, I feel the gratitude, and that feeling I created back in Gloucester of "I LOVE my life"— long before I knew this life existed.

Use your Touchstone to keep you focused on the feeling of the result you want, without thinking about the details or even the result itself. Just the feeling. And keep repeating it—no matter where you are, right now.

When you're traveling to a destination, you know you're going to end up in that destination. Even if there are diversions and delays along the way, you may feel annoyed or disappointed, but you don't doubt that you're going to end up there. The Touchstone helps to cut out the noise from delays, storms, diversions, and corners around which you can't see. It helps to keep you focused on the end result, even as the route appears to take you in different directions from the one you expected. As long as that feeling is the feeling you want to experience, and you keep "touching" that Touchstone to keep yourself on track, regardless of what's going on in the meantime, you will end up there.

I feel like a person from the 18th century who wanted to get from A to B faster, and who really, really wanted a horse, because a horse was the only thing I knew about. And then, I was presented with a sports car. Something I couldn't have wished for because I had no idea they existed. I had no way of knowing that the life I live now would be the life I love. Because I had no way of seeing it from where I was back then.

RECAP:

- A Touchstone is a moment in time that can represent how you'll feel when you have what you want.
- It's important to not include any details—it's just a feeling and a phrase, with no specifics. This will help you to keep your focus on the end feeling rather than having intruding doubts, fears, and distractions.
- The more you "touch" that Touchstone, the more you'll stay on the road to your desired destination.

In addition to using your Touchstone, be sure to also keep changing the negative childhood memories to the opposite, positive, and empowering, and practicing the new ones. Your Touchstone keeps your vehicle pointed in the direction of your desired destination, but you need to make sure your GPS is programmed for that destination, too. You may also find that some of those memories will need Stepping-Stones...

Chapter 19

Check Engine Light: Stepping-Stone Memories

M emories are not stored as pictures or movies, and they're not stored in one particular place in the brain. The information is stored throughout the brain and pulled together as we recall something.

> *"When faced with a choice, the brain retrieves specific traces of memories, rather than a generalized overview of past experiences, from its mental Rolodex, according to new brain-imaging research from The University of Texas at Austin."*
> —"New study decodes brain's process for decision making." ScienceDaily[60].

The fact that, when faced with a choice, the brain pulls traces of different memories, rather than a full story, is the reason we use Stepping-Stone Memories.

When to Use Stepping-Stone Memories

A Stepping-Stone Memory is used to address different (often contradicting) data from one memory. Each Stepping-Stone Memory is separate

---

60   University of Texas at Austin. "New study decodes brain's process for decision making." ScienceDaily. November 2013. www.sciencedaily.com/releases/2013/11/131108112144.htm.

and stands alone. We can use these separate new bits of data in Stepping-Stone Memories because the unconscious part of the brain doesn't need the continuity of a logical storyline.

For example:

If you were bullied in school, and when you told your parents, they didn't support you, the final memory you need to aim for is:

Instead of being bullied, you were popular. All the other kids admired you and wanted to be friends with you. You now have memories of the other kids arguing over who gets to sit next to you, bringing you gifts, and wanting you on their sports teams. You now have memories of everyone wanting you at their party, and so on.

Stepping-Stone Memories:

If you just created those final memories, that would be good—and better than the old ones, of course—but it would not be enough. There would still be old data to do with not being protected by adults, no one standing up for you, being powerless to stand up for yourself, not being believed, and possibly more, depending on your particular experience and the existing references from before you were bullied.

Stepping-Stone Memories address and change each of those separate pieces of data:

Stepping-Stone One:

You were still bullied, but when you told your parents, they were horrified, and immediately protective of you. They hugged you, reassured you, and then went to the school, and confronted the teacher and/or the principal and/or the bullies and/or the bullies' parents. You could have the bullies expelled, or even arrested. Whatever that little you wished would happen.

Depending on what's already there, this Stepping-Stone addresses feeling safe, valued, protected, heard, loved, being believed, and allowed to speak out.

Repeat that first Stepping-Stone until it feels established then move on to Stepping-Stone Two.

Stepping-Stone Two:
You were still bullied, but a teacher saw what was happening, and stopped it. The bullies were confronted, punished, and remorseful.

This step addresses being safe: someone's looking out for you, you're valuable, you're noticed, someone's got your back, you're not alone, and you are worth standing up for. There may be different or additional data, depending on existing references and, of course, the bullying experience itself.

Stepping-Stone Three:
The bullies start to bully, but you stand up for yourself. It could be verbally or physically defending yourself—or both. Whatever will empower that little you. You could even give that little you a magic wand to defend or protect yourself with. Remember that the unconscious part of your brain can't tell the difference between reality and imagination, can't use logic or reason, and can't judge something as unrealistic—it will believe whatever you give it. This Stepping-Stone addresses feeling empowered, strong, respected, safe, and confident.

A very important piece of these memories is that the bullies are remorseful, apologetic, and respectful.

You could add other Stepping-Stones depending on what stands out from the original event.

For one of our clients, a key piece of the original experience was dreading going to school and begging her mother to allow her to not have to go back. In her case, in addition to the Stepping-Stones above, we added one where she tells her mother she doesn't want to go back to that school, and her mother agrees, kindly, compassionately, and supportively: *"Of course, sweetheart, you don't have to go back. You can stay home, and we'll find a nicer school for you. You never have to do anything you don't want to do."*

Do you see how that creates a different feeling to the other Stepping-Stones? It was a very important factor in that client being able to move forward. It was also, of course, a foundation for a pattern in her life as an adult—of having to do other things she didn't want to. Feeling she didn't want to go to work, but had to, for example.

Practice each Stepping-Stone until it feels established, and then you can move on to the Final Memory, which would be that the negative event never happened in the first place, and instead, something wonderful happened.

For example:

Instead of being bullied, you're the most popular kid in school.

Instead of being physically harmed, you're now swimming, on a trampoline, on a funfair ride, playing a fun game, doing a fun activity, meeting a celebrity…and everyone is kind, compassionate, safe, and fun.

Instead of losing something, you are receiving something even better.

Instead of being told terrible news, you're being told you're all going to Disneyworld, or that you're getting a pony, or something else exciting.

An example from Steve:

Like many of us, I was also someone who experienced being bullied on the playground. The apex of this bullying occurred when I was about 11 years old. A new boy had joined our school and he quickly asserted himself at the top of the pecking order. Being unathletic and leaning more toward the creative and the artistic, I soon found myself the number one pariah of this newly created fiefdom, and daily on the receiving end of verbal and physical abuse by the new schoolyard bully and his minions.

As I engaged in the work of transforming this memory, I found that I could not gain a sense of peace with the new memory. I had written a Due Justice letter to the bully, and I had created a new empowering memory of him and I becoming friends, however, it just felt "off." It was a story that I could recite, but it didn't feel entirely real.

In spending more time investigating these feelings, and what was still providing a tether to the feelings of the original bullying memories, I discovered a feeling of being helpless and defenseless. This was the piece of conflicting data that made the new story of being friends incompatible. So, I created a Stepping-Stone Memory for that disempowered 11-year-old version of myself. I imagined the adult me taking that little me to martial arts training.

During this time of changing that memory, I was also making a 40-minute daily commute to work, which provided a great built-in block of time to rehearse the new Stepping-Stone Memory. I spent a few weeks enjoying this newfound power as the new 11-year-old karate master walked through the playground, using his skills to slam the bully and henchmen to the ground. I allowed myself to feel the power of being able to protect myself and others.

After this feeling of power was established, I was able to return to the new memory of the new boy (former bully) and I becoming best friends, and this time it felt believable and real, and I found that I could imagine even more endearing details.

What Do Stepping-Stones Do?

Since the brain refers to specific *traces* of memory, rather than whole memories, to find out what an experience means and how to respond, it's important to change those separate pieces of the memory and their associated meanings. As you then create each Stepping-Stone, you change those specific pieces of data and the meaning they represent.

For example, if you'd told an adult that you were bullied, and that adult didn't believe you, there will be some data (depending on what other references are there as well) that "proves" something else about your self-image and worldview. For example, it may be "evidence" that you're not worthy, or that you're alone in this world, or that no one will help you, or that you don't have a right to complain, or that you don't have a voice, or that it's dangerous to speak up for yourself... The possibilities are endless, and they will be a combination of the data from all the childhood experiences you went through.

On the other hand, if you were to make the final memory one where you speak up, and you're protected by the adult, you would still have the bullying piece of that experience (which, again, means something to your brain about who you are and how the world works). Both aspects of the experience need changing.

Having changed the references for being protected, so it's now safe to stand up for yourself, and you have the power to defend and protect yourself, the final memory can be the ideal, which is that you were never bullied—and, in fact, you were the most popular kid in school. Everyone loved you, looked up to you, respected you, admired you, and wanted to be with you.

It's important to remember that the unconscious part of the brain that refers to these childhood memories does not understand linear time and cannot use logic or reason—it cannot understand stories. It's all just pieces of data that "prove" who you are and how the world works. So, if you were to choose a Stepping-Stone as a final memory—for example, when the bully tried to harm you, but you had the strength to defend yourself—the unconscious part of your brain isn't able to put that together as an outcome. When we *reason* that it all worked out, we're using the cortex (the conscious, thinking part of the brain), but it isn't the conscious part that is running the show on automatic. It's the unconscious part of the brain that refers to those "specific traces of memory" without the story. And it is that unconscious part of the brain that triggers our automatic reactions.

So, for example, you may then experience being able to speak up for yourself in a relationship or at work (your brain now refers to those childhood memories of it being safe to speak up), but you may still constantly find yourself in situations where you're triggered and are having to speak up (your brain will still refer to the fact that there are people who want to hurt you). And it will affect your judgment, decision-making, and perception, so that you're unconsciously attracted to situations and people where you will feel that "normal" state of *they want to hurt me,* or *life is unfair,* or *I'm not safe,* or whatever else is still there.

Stepping-Stones replace the extra pieces of negative and disempowering data while still keeping the final memory the ultimate experience.

How to Use Stepping-Stone Memories

Start by asking yourself what the worst things are about the original memory. What things stand out for you in terms of feelings, emotions, actions, lack of action, or other people's reactions?

Then imagine each part of that memory as a separate piece of data and ask yourself what would have been the most empowering experience in that moment. For example, if your pet died, and one of the worst things about that situation was not being able to do anything—feeling helpless—what would it have been like if you had been empowered to do something? Give that little you a magic wand and have them "magic" the pet alive again.

Remind yourself that the unconscious part of your brain that is referring to these memories can't judge something as unrealistic, can't use logic or reason—doesn't know, for example, that magic isn't real—and won't question it. It will believe whatever you give it. The only part of you that questions logically is your conscious mind, and you have control over that. Whatever you give that unconscious part of your brain, it will believe.

The only reason that the unconscious part of your brain will object to a new memory is if it holds other memories that contradict it, memories that it can't change automatically. If that's the case, you'll find that something pops into your mind (it may appear to be completely random—remember, there's no logic to the unconscious part of your brain and the connections it makes) and then you can change that to the opposite, positive, and empowering, as well.

RECAP:

- Memories are not stories in the brain—they are stored as pieces of data, providing references for different aspects of our self-image and worldview.
- While the conscious mind can use reason regarding specific events, the unconscious part of the brain is not able to connect those dots.
- Stepping-Stone Memories address the different pieces of data within a particular memory.

But what if you can't find any memories?

What if, your answer to Detective Question 3 (from Chapter 5): *Where in your childhood did you feel this same feeling?* is: *I don't know?*

There's Nothing There: Extra Detective Work

As we explained in Chapter 5, the three main Detective Questions to ask yourself, that will help you to find the particular childhood memories that provide the foundation for specific issues you want to change, are:

1. How do I know (or what's the worst thing about it)?
2. How does that feel?
3. Where, in my childhood, did I feel that same feeling (it may be a different topic but will be the same feeling)?

In addition to these questions, there are several other approaches to finding the childhood memories that are causing the challenges you're experiencing as an adult.

When to Use the Extra Detective Work

You may find that there are times when the answer to Detective Question 3: *Where in my childhood did I feel this feeling?* is: *"I don't know."* If no memory comes up from childhood, you can ask yourself the extra Detective Questions in this chapter.

What Does it Do?

The Extra Detective Work is designed to trigger different connections in your brain, to retrieve information you may not have access to having tried the other questions and techniques. Think of it as searching in different places on your computer for a particular file. You start by typing the name you think you gave the file into the search box for the folder you believe you saved it to. If nothing comes up, you may try typing in different words, or search on your Desktop or in other folders, and you may do a search of your hard drive. These extra Detective Questions are the equivalent of typing different words into the search box, and searching the whole computer for the file, in case it's saved under a different name.

How to Use Extra Detective Work

First, ask yourself the three main questions:

1. How do I know (or what's the worst thing about it)?
2. How does that feel?
3. Where, in my childhood, did I feel this same feeling (it may be a different topic, but will be the same feeling)?

You can then ask the following questions to find extra links and information that your brain may have connected to the issue you want to change:

1. **If this problem were a person, who would it be?**
    If it represents a person from your adult life, ask yourself who that person reminds you of, from your childhood. Then, change the negative memories of that person. For example: *"If money were a person, it would be my boss. My boss reminds me of my mother."* Change the negative memories of your mother, first, to the opposite, positive, and empowering. Even if your negative experiences with money and with your boss feel stronger, it is your childhood references of your mother that are providing the "evidence" that

"proves" how you experience money and your boss. So, those childhood memories of your mother need to be changed first.

2. **Who or what does this person or experience remind me of?**
   Again, if it reminds you of something or someone from your adult life, ask yourself what that person or experience reminds you of from your childhood, and change that first.

3. **What does this experience or issue mean to me? And where in my childhood did I experience that meaning?**
   Everything we experience—regardless of the situation, circumstances, events, and people involved—is determined by the references we hold. As we experience something, the unconscious part of the brain refers to data from previous experiences to find out what this current experience means, and how to respond. The conscious mind is not involved in this process. In fact, the conscious mind doesn't become aware of the response until after it's happened automatically.

An example from a client:

In our online daily group session, one of our clients shared that she was fed up with a neighbor playing loud music. The neighbor had moved in recently and was playing music loudly on her balcony. Angela felt triggered and frustrated, as well as helpless. She couldn't sit on her own balcony and enjoy her own music, and she couldn't see how she could resolve this issue.

Her answer to this question: What does this experience or issue mean to me? was:

"She thinks she's the only one in the world." Angela's main experience of this neighbor was the fact that she was selfish and didn't care about the effects of her actions on others. She was just doing what she wanted to do, without concern for anyone else.

Her answer to the rest of the question: "Where in my childhood did I experience this feeling?" was her sister. Angela's childhood was filled with experiences of a selfish sibling. As she was forced to listen to the loud music, Angela's brain was referring to memories of suffering due to her sister's selfishness. Along with other references, those memories of her sister being selfish were the closest match her brain had to this experience with the neighbor.

Instantly, her brain then pumped stress chemicals into her system, which caused those same feelings to surface of being at the mercy of a selfish person while she was helpless to do anything about it. And as her conscious mind became aware of those feelings, it did its job—it assigned meaning to those feelings. The neighbor playing that loud music was the visible, obvious reason. And as Angela thought about the neighbor's lack of concern for others, those thoughts, again, triggered yet more stress chemicals…and so it became a cycle of amping up feelings of frustration and helplessness.

The goal was to change those memories of her sister to ones where her sister was kind, loving, considerate, and always put Angela first. In these new memories, her sister doted on her, just like her parents did in her new memories of them. And then, her experience of her neighbor would change—from being an emotional trigger, to being something she either doesn't mind anymore or something she knows how to deal with. With her prefrontal cortex back online (because she's no longer emotionally triggered), she would be able to think of options and solutions she hadn't been able to think of before. No longer feeling helpless would open her mind to being able to think of strategic solutions.

Update: As it happens, after Angela changed those childhood memories, her neighbor seems to have found a distraction, and is no longer playing music on her balcony.

4.   **If this doesn't change, what's the worst thing that could happen? What am I most worried about? What does that remind me of from childhood?**

An example from Odille:

I was giving a free talk at an event in Cheltenham, in the UK, and I had copies of my second book with me. It was a tiny audience, probably around 15 people, and afterward, someone came up and asked me how much my book was. I felt the familiar feelings of fear and awkwardness and wanting to cringe. I said, "Oh, no, don't worry," and gave her the book without payment.

I remember going into a state of extreme fear whenever I thought about asking to be paid or asking for work. In fact, asking for anything. I used to sing in pubs, and afterward, I would feel an intense freezing fear when it came to asking them for the money they'd agreed to pay me. I would sit and wait and hope they would come and pay me without my needing to ask. Since the management and staff were busy serving customers, and since most entertainers asked for their money, it's not something that usually happened. So, I would eventually make myself go up and ask, feeling cringey and fearful for no evident reason.

So, I asked myself: What's the worst thing about asking for something? The answer was: It feels like I'm doing something wrong and something bad is going to happen if I ask for something from someone else. Where in my childhood did I feel that same feeling? A phrase came to my mind. I had completely forgotten about it until I asked myself that question. "If you ask, you don't get." It's something we'd been taught as part of being polite.

My family was very strict about manners, politeness, and being considerate of others. The problem with being taught to put others first is the knock-on effect of that politeness and consideration: the message to the unconscious part of the brain that others are more important than us. And (depending on what other references are formed) it can become one of the foundations of an inability to prioritize self-care.

"May I have a cookie?"

"Well, now that you've asked, you can't have it. You wait to be offered."

Not all children's brains will learn to apply that "logic" across the board, but the combination of references in my brain from my experiences as a child to that point created an unconscious belief that if I asked for anything, I wasn't going to get it.

As an adult, when I thought about asking for work, or asking to be paid, (or in some cases, even just asking what time it was) that unconscious part of my brain still referred to the "evidence"—the "fact"—that if I ask, I won't get. And it then triggered the stress chemicals that would result in fear, so that I wouldn't ask. But I was completely unaware of this. The phrase: "If you ask, you don't get," wasn't in my mind, consciously. I hadn't thought of it since I was a child. So, I had no idea why I was so frightened to ask as an adult.

Of course, it makes no logical sense. It's one thing when you're teaching children manners, but it's completely impractical for an adult. In reality, if you don't ask, you're less likely to get. As we think about that logic, we use the part of the brain that can use logic and reason. But that's not the part of the brain that responds to experiences. The unconscious part of the brain that was triggering the emergency response inside me whenever I thought about asking for something, is unable to use logic or reason. It was just responding according to what it was "programmed" with, automatically, and with no more logical thought than a dog who barks at a passerby.

I changed that reference by creating new childhood memories of being taught, instead: "It's safe to ask for what you want," and "If you want something, it's good to ask for it." New memories of being encouraged with kindness, compassion, affection, and fun, to ask for things. And new memories of me asking for things, and the adult smiling and saying, "Of course!" clearly happy to give me what I asked for. I created new memories of going into a store with my mum, my dad, and each of my grandparents, and that little me pointing at a toy, asking for it, and the adult buying it for me.

After creating those new memories and establishing them by repeating them, with all of the associated good feelings, I no longer feel fear when I ask for something. The fear has been replaced with kindness, consideration, and love.

5. **What *good* memories do I have from childhood that remind me of this issue or person?**

    Although negative memories form most of the references that contribute to the issues we experience as adults, there are some issues (often, addiction) that are supported by good memories—where the brain has made an unconscious link between a particular substance, behavior, or type of person, and a feeling of love, connection, or safety.

An example from Odille:

The first time I worked with someone who wanted to stop smoking, back in 2016, we found a link between love and connection, and smoking. We'd addressed some of the negative memories from her childhood, and then I asked her: "Do you have any good memories about smoking?" Her daughter and husband smoked, and the three of them would stand in the yard, outside the kitchen door, smoking together, and drinking soda. The feeling in these memories was a connection with each other. Smiles, love, fun, and connection.

When I asked her what it reminded her of, from her childhood, she remembered that her grandfather smoked. She had memories of sitting with him on the steps in front of the house while he had a cigarette. Her grandfather was calm and kind, and funny—a sharp contrast to her own father—and she felt close to him, and safe with him.

So, her brain had connected the smell of cigarettes with feelings of love, connection, and feeling safe. When she smelled cigarettes, or just thought about them, her brain would refer to that "evidence" that "proved" it means safety, connection, fun, and love, and it would then trigger the "feel-good" chemicals that create those feelings of connection, love, and feeling safe for her.

In addition to changing negative childhood memories to the opposite, positive, and empowering, here's how we changed those original references with her grandfather:

I asked her to think about one of those memories of sitting on the steps with her grandfather, with him smoking, and to allow herself to really home in on the feeling of love, connection, and safety, to notice what it was she loved about her grandfather. Once she could feel those feelings, I asked her to take the cigarette out of the scene, and replace it with a glass of iced water, with the ice blocks tinkling in it. Then, I asked her what scent she loves. She mentioned a few options, including the smell of the sea. So, I asked her to add the ocean. In her new memories, she and her grandfather are now sitting on the front steps of a beachfront house, drinking glasses of iced water, with the sounds and smell of the ocean in the background.

Now, her brain has healthier connections in that particular reference, as well as new childhood memories that "prove" she was loved, safe, and connected with her parents—and she no longer wants to smoke.

6. **How was I punished, as a child, when I did something wrong?**
   When a client says, *"But I had a good childhood. No trauma, I knew my parents loved me, and I felt safe,"* a question that often uncovers unexpected references for unwanted issues is: How were you punished when you did something wrong? The first time we asked this question, the client said, *"I was beaten with a belt—but I deserved it. I was a nightmare child."*

   Punishment—regardless of how "justified"—can create powerful core "evidence" for a range of issues we experience as adults. Just the phrase *"I deserved it"* can be the foundation of a variety of struggles and suffering in all areas of life.

   Remember that the conscious mind can use reason and logic like: *"My parents did the best they could. Punishing me was the only way they knew to keep me safe. They punished me because they loved me. I was a very difficult child and punishing me was the only way to get me under control..."* All of that may be true. But the unconscious part of the brain that interprets experiences and converts them into implicit memory—"evidence" that "proves" who we are and how the world works—has no ability to use logic or reason. It has no ability to connect those dots.

   It would be like trying to explain to a dog why he has to get in the car to go to the vet, and that afterwards, you'll take him to the park. The dog is reacting to a trigger, followed by chemicals in his system, and doesn't have the ability to understand reasoning. He cannot comprehend time, logic, or reason, and is not capable of any other cognitive understanding. The unconscious part of the human brain that determines our perception, experience, and responses in life is the same.

   When we experience punishment as a child, the conscious part of the brain may understand it as a consequence of our actions and choices, and that our parents had no other option...but the unconscious part of the brain will interpret it to mean something about who we are and how the world works, depending on the other references that are already there from previous experiences.

If you were punished at all, in any way (this applies to all types of punishment, from corporal punishment to "time out" to being denied outings or privileges to "the silent treatment")—for anything—change those memories. Depending on the original memories, add Stepping-Stone Memories that address the separate pieces of data.

For example:

Stepping-Stone One: You were able to stop the punishment. You had a magic wand, or you were able to speak out and make the person stop and listen to you. Then, instead of punishing you, they understand and acknowledge you.

Stepping-Stone Two: There is no punishment in the first place. You are never punished. When you do something wrong, they sit down with you and explain what you need to do differently next time—and how to create a strategy to achieve that.

Final Memory: You never did anything wrong. And instead of whatever it was you did wrong in the original memory, now you are being praised for something wonderful you did. You're showing your parents your 100% score on an exam, or the amazing artwork you created, or you're telling them that you've been chosen to represent your school in an exciting event, or you're demonstrating a physical activity you've achieved. And your parents are so proud of you, they're beaming. They're fully focused on you and tell you how lucky they are to have you. They hug you and tell you how much they love you and how proud they are of you.

Remember: The unconscious part of your brain will believe whatever you give it. So, if, as you imagine that you never did anything wrong and your parents were proud of you, resistance pops up, such as: *But all children do things wrong—that's part of being a* *child,* or *My parents would never have had the time to sit down and explain everything to me*—remind yourself that those thoughts are coming from your *conscious, logical* mind. The unconscious part of your brain has no ability to think that way. It's like the dog, living in the moment, with no ability to comprehend logic, reason, or even time. It will believe the new memories, as long as you allow it to, if you answer those objections from the conscious mind.

RECAP:

- When you can't find negative childhood memories in answer to: *Where did I experience this same feeling in my childhood?* use the Extra Detective Questions to uncover the roots of the issues you want to change.
- The original childhood references for current issues can sometimes be rooted in positive memories. Keep the positive, and replace the negative aspect with a healthier, more empowering option (e.g. replacing cigarettes with iced water and the smell of the ocean).
- Remember that being punished as a child can be providing the "evidence" of the issues you want to change. Even if the conscious mind understands, the unconscious part of the brain cannot use that reasoning. Change all memories of punishment using Stepping-Stones and end with a final memory that you never did anything wrong.

There will be times when a memory won't seem to change—or part of it won't change. In that case, there may be an Anchor Memory…

Not This Again!
Anchor Memories

W e've found that when a person can't seem to imagine a memory differently, it's sometimes because there are other references (implicit memories) that are "holding it in place." Think of it this way: If you imagine a memory differently, the unconscious part of your brain will believe whatever you give it—*except* if there's other strong evidence that "proves" it would be dangerous to change that memory. The tricky part is that, because that unconscious part of your brain doesn't use logic or reason, the connection between the memory you're trying to change, and the Anchor Memory may make no sense at all to the conscious mind. Changing the Anchor Memory will remove that "danger" and allow you to change the rest.

> "We don't innately know what a pencil, tuna salad sandwich, or a bicycle is. We have to learn what these are, and later use the memories we form to recognize them."[61]
>
> —Joseph E. LeDoux, Henry and Lucy Moses, professor of science at NYU in the Center for Neural Science, director of the Emotional Brain Institute of NYU and the Nathan Kline Institute.

When to Look for Anchor Memories

When you've changed a memory, but the new memory still has something about it from the old experience, or it doesn't feel complete, it may be because there's an Anchor Memory in place.

The Effects of Finding and Changing Anchor Memories

Think about changing a memory as being like sailing a boat. If the boat won't move, you know there's an anchor somewhere, holding it in place. This process helps you to find the anchor. You must walk around the deck and notice where the chain is, then follow the chain that holds the anchor to find the anchor and lift it. Once you've lifted the anchor, the boat can move. If it still won't move, it means there's another anchor somewhere, and you repeat the process until you're able to move the boat.

In other words, if you can't imagine a memory differently, you can use this process to follow the trail to find the memory that is holding that one in place. Once you find it, you can change it, and then check if the "boat will move" (if you can change the original memory to the opposite, positive, and empowering). If you still can't imagine that first memory differently, it means there's another anchor. So, repeat the process until you're able to imagine that memory differently.

How to Find Anchor Memories

1. When you can't imagine a negative memory differently by changing it to the opposite, positive, and empowering, ask yourself: *"What happens when I try?"*
2. Notice what stands out to you. Even if it seems odd and doesn't make any sense.
3. As you think about that particular aspect that stands out to you, ask yourself what it reminds you of, from your childhood.
4. Take notice of the first thing that pops into your mind, even if it seems completely random to the logical mind and makes no sense. If it's coming up, your brain has linked it.

5. Change that memory to the opposite, positive, and empowering, and then come back to the memory you were trying to change and see if you're able to "move the boat" now. In other words, see if you're able to imagine that memory differently, now. If not, repeat steps 1 to 5, until you're able to change the memory to the opposite, positive, and empowering.

6. Repeat the new memory until it's established.

An example from Odille:

The first time I discovered this process, I was working with a client who had changed a negative memory of being locked out of her home, in the snow, as a child. She had changed the memory to where, instead of the snow, it was a field of flowers, and she was playing in the flowers. But there was still something from the old memory that wouldn't change. There was still some negative emotion.

I asked her what stood out for her, and she said it was a piece of wall of the house. The rest was a field of flowers, but there was this piece of wall in the field that she couldn't move in her mind. Of course, bearing in mind that thoughts are connections between neurons in our own brains, we have control over what we think about, so when we can't change something in our own imaginations, it means there's something else holding it in place.

It made no sense to her, as she didn't know what the wall represented, and she didn't have any other memories related to a wall. I asked her, as she focused on that piece of wall, what it reminded her of, from her childhood and to tell me the first thing that popped into her mind, even if it made no sense. She told me of an experience that had nothing to do with a wall and didn't even take place at the house. It was a memory of a babysitter dragging her across a road when she wanted to stop and look at something.

It seemed random and completely unconnected to the original memory she was trying to change (which didn't involve a babysitter and was nowhere near a road) and there seemed to be no logical reason why these two experiences were connected. But the fact that the second one had come up meant that her brain had not only connected them, but that there was something about the second memory that her brain was holding on to as "proof" it would be dangerous to change the first memory.

I talked her through changing the memory of the babysitter, using a Stepping-Stone where the babysitter wanted her to cross the road, she said she wanted to look at something, and the babysitter agreed. This is the final new memory she came up with: A giraffe had appeared in the town, and she and the babysitter stopped to look at it and play with it.

Once she'd imagined this new memory and established it by repeating it a few times, we went back to the first memory—the field of flowers. The piece of wall that was there before had gone, along with the negative feeling. That memory was now that little girl, playing in a beautiful field of flowers, with a wonderful feeling.

This session took place a few years ago. I would now suggest adding her parents to that new memory—creating the connection, love, and safety between them. So that instead of being locked out of the house in the snow, alone, she and her parents are playing in a field of flowers, having fun.

Random

Note that an Anchor Memory often appears to have no logical connection to the memory you're trying to change. Go with whatever pops into your mind, first. No matter how random or unlikely it may seem, change it anyway.

RECAP:

- Anchor Memories are the references your brain is holding on to that "prove" it would be dangerous to change the memory you're trying to change.
- The connection between the memory you're trying to change, and the Anchor Memory may well make no logical sense at all, but if it's coming up, it's connected.

In addition to finding and changing Anchor Memories, check what your childhood experiences were of your culture, history, and religion. In Chapter 23, we'll address the effects of heritage and tradition on a person's self-image and worldview—and how to change them.

Chapter 22

Who Said That?
Answering Self-Talk

Try saying this phrase, right now, as if you're speaking to the child inside you: *"I see you, I hear you, I feel you, I love you."*

Whenever you're speaking to yourself, you are speaking to the child in you. Whenever you're feeling doubt, fear, anger, frustration, disappointment, it's coming from the child in you.

You've Adopted the Little You

We all have doubts and negative thoughts. And we have them far more frequently than we may realize! The key is to *answer* those thoughts and feelings. Rather than just going along with them, and joining in, or ignoring them, answer as if you're answering a child who just expressed that thought. Because it is the child in you who is feeling that feeling.

Imagine you adopted a child who had the background and childhood experiences you had. Each of us has adopted the child we were, from our parents. Those who raised us are no longer raising us—*we* are now raising us. We are now the only one in charge of that child. We take over from where those who raised us left off but, interestingly, we tend to treat ourselves—automatically and unconsciously—in the same way as those who raised us treated us.

Notice how you treat the child when they're feeling frightened, angry, frustrated, not good enough. Do you agree with them? If a child were to say something like *I'm so stupid,* would you agree? Would you add all the reasons that child is stupid? Or would you reassure the child, and tell them they're perfect and have always done the best they can with what they had? And would you help them to make different choices and remember things, and improve, moving forward, in a kind, productive, creative, encouraging way?

When that child says something like, *I'll never achieve my goal,* would you agree with them, and add all the reasons they won't achieve their goal? Would you point out all the previous times they've failed, and the fact that they never follow through? Or would you answer that child with reassurance, encouragement, and enthusiasm? Would you point out reasons they *can* achieve their goal, and help them with strategies to do what it takes to get there?

When you notice negative thoughts and feelings, answer them! Answer them as if a child is telling you that thought or feeling. This practice alone can completely change your life—not only by how you feel, but by what you achieve. The fact that all negative emotions cause stress chemicals, and stress chemicals cause the cognitive-thinking part of your brain to go offline, means that when you catch those negative thoughts and feelings early—and answer them the way you would answer a child—with encouragement, kindness, compassion, and reassurance—you will come up with ideas, opportunities, solutions, strategies, and creativity you couldn't have found without that part of your brain online. You'll make different decisions and will come up with different ideas that will lead to different results. You'll find yourself taking different actions, communicating differently, willing to do different things that help you to achieve your goals.

An example from Odille:

During 2016, when I started changing my negative childhood memories, I was on a bit of a rollercoaster. Life was so much better than it had been, and I was doing better, financially, than I'd ever done, but there were still big hurdles and challenges ahead.

The increase in my income was coming from writing for clients. And I loved that work. However, around the middle of the year, my biggest client started reducing the amount of work they gave me, and then stopped hiring me altogether. They were happy with my writing but had found a much cheaper writer. About a month after that, another client put the work I was doing for them on hold. My first thoughts were of going backward. Just when I thought I had changed my life, now I was going to end up back in the rented room in the shared house, cleaning other people's houses and unable to pay my bills. It felt like the old familiar pattern was repeating itself.

You Can't See Around Corners

In the past, I would have followed those thoughts and feelings, buying into them, thinking about all the reasons I'd failed. Why does this always happen? What had I done wrong? I could already feel the increase in my heart rate and the extreme fear building. But I answered. I answered those thoughts and feelings as I would if it was someone else who was confiding in me about these fears and doubts. I spoke to myself as I would a friend—reassuringly: "Just because you can't see the road ahead doesn't mean there isn't one." I used the little exercise from Part One of this book and practiced the new memories. I reminded myself that as long as I made sure the GPS coordinates matched the destination I wanted to reach and I practiced "staying on the road" using the techniques we've shared with you in this book, it had to all work out perfectly.

I reminded myself that we can't see around corners. Just because I couldn't see another way to make an income, didn't mean there wasn't one. I reminded myself that bringing my prefrontal cortex back online, by lowering the levels of stress chemicals and increasing the levels of "feel-good" chemicals, would automatically allow me to see new opportunities, think of solutions, and be creative. Every time the feelings and thoughts of doubt and fear (and they were very strong and persistent) came up, I answered them in the same way I would answer someone else—with reassurance, logic, and kindness.

Once I had brought down the intensity of the fear and doubt, and I was feeling better, I asked myself the three Detective Questions:

1. How do I know? How do I know that I'm going backward, and going to end up in the same financial struggle I was in before?

I know because this is what always happens. Every time I think everything's going well, and I get excited about something, something happens to take me back to the state of struggle.

2. How does that feel?

It feels like I'm not allowed to get excited about things going well. It feels like I wanted too much… And, suddenly, my grandmother popped into my mind. And the word "greedy" came up.

3. So, where did I experience that same feeling in my childhood? (It may be a different topic but will be the same feeling.)

My grandmother had a thing about people being greedy. She had suffered so much in her life, and she'd also witnessed a lot of suffering in others. And her view on life, of course, came from her own references of greedy people taking from others. This was a powerful theme throughout my childhood.

It made perfect sense. As I was changing my childhood references, and therefore my financial situation, continuing to plan improvements for *my life, the unconscious part of my brain was referring to the "danger" of being greedy. If I was greedy, my grandmother would hate me, which, to that survival part of the brain, would mean death. This was what created the doubt and fear in me, not the loss of my writing client.*

As I changed those memories to the opposite, positive, and empowering, I felt a surge of love, peace, joy, and connection with my grandmother. Practicing those new memories to establish them, I found my mind automatically coming up with creative ideas and solutions. About a week later, I had created my first free email course. From there, I started helping others, using what I had discovered, and I realized that if I hadn't lost the writing clients, I may never have built my own business. I would have continued working for others, writing about their work, instead of pioneering, developing, and creating my own. And this book would not exist!

It's important to notice that it was answering that self-talk—answering my doubts and fears—that enabled me to do the rest. It was using logic and reason—my conscious mind—to answer those doubts and fears, compassionately, as I would someone else, that enabled me to keep the stress chemicals from getting too high to be able to use the little exercise from Part One. And from there I was able to find and change the references that were creating the fear and doubt and therefore gain access to the cognitive-thinking part of my brain that allowed me to be creative and to problem-solve, instead of staying in a perpetual state of fear.

When to Use Answering Self-Talk

Every time you become aware that you've said or thought something negative to, or about, yourself, answer it. Every time you notice a negative observation, a doubt, or a fear, recognize that what you're

experiencing in that moment is coming from the child you've adopted—
the little you—and answer the way you would answer if that child were
in the room with you.

RECAP:

- The doubts, fears, and other negative thoughts and feelings that
  crop up come from the unconscious part of the brain.
- Using the conscious part of the brain to answer those thoughts
  and feelings helps to keep your prefrontal cortex (the cognitive-
  thinking part of your brain) online. And that, of course, affects
  everything.

Now it's time to make a stop at the Roadside Museum...

Rewriting Culture or Religion

If, when you think of your culture or religious background, you feel love, security, connection, and reassurance, of course you want to keep that feeling. On the other hand, if you have negative, disempowering feelings, be aware that those references may be contributing to the challenges you're experiencing. Just as negative childhood memories can be changed, you can also change the references in your subconscious to do with culture and religion.

How would you answer this question? *"I come from a long line of _____."*

You want that sentence to end with everything you want in your life, now. Just like you want your GPS coordinates to match your desired destination. So, if your current answer to the question above is something like: *"I come from a long line of people who suffered / struggled / were persecuted / were hard-working / lived in poverty / were fighters / were betrayed…"* what you're aiming to end up with is something like: *"I come from a long line of people who were joyful, kind, compassionate, fun, safe, enthusiastic, loving, connected, abundant, loved by all…"* and anything else you want to experience in your life, now.

Remember: You are not changing history, and you are not denying your heritage or rejecting your background. You are changing implicit memory to declarative memory. You are changing the unconscious references that "prove" who you are and how the world works, automatically— references that "prove" you have to continue to suffer the way your ancestors suffered—to conscious memories that you can access whenever needed. But they will no longer automatically "prove" the results you don't want in your life. You are changing the "evidence" that "proves" who you are and how the world works so that it "proves" what you *want* to experience in your life, moving forward. You aren't denying you've been in the city, you are changing the GPS coordinates to the beach, so that while you can still remember you *were* in the city, you are now automatically being guided to the destination you want to end up in.

Dealing with Ongoing Injustice and Suffering

Life can be especially challenging when you're dealing with ongoing injustice and suffering. The purpose of using the knowledge and techniques in this book is to empower the individual—to empower you. And empowerment comes from within. Whatever's going on around you, if you can do something to change it right now, then, of course, go ahead and do that. But if you can't, feeling helpless and hopeless won't help you, or any others who are suffering. What can help is this:

1. Gaining control over your own brain chemistry so that you have access to your cognitive thinking (your problem-solving skills, your ability to process information, your creativity, and your communication skills) so that you can use strategy to find opportunities and solutions you may not have thought of before.
2. Changing your own childhood memories, and your own family history to prove the results you want to create in your life.

From there, you may find that instead of feeling the pain of injustice, persecution, and other suffering that you have no control over, you are able to come up with options, solutions, and ideas from a place of empowerment, rather than a place of struggle.

When to Rewrite Culture or Religion

If you're finding it difficult to change your negative childhood memories, or your parents' or grandparents' childhood memories, it may be because of the references from your cultural or religious background. Notice what happens when you try to use the Generational Childhood Memory Transformation technique. What thoughts, feelings, and memories come up that prevent you from imagining your parents and grandparents growing up feeling safe, loved, and valued, treated kindly and compassionately, encouraged, respected, and supported? If you find thoughts, feelings, or memories that are rooted in culture, history, or religion, you can use this technique to change those references.

An example from Steve:

One of the first times I used this technique was when I worked with a client from Northern Ireland. We had spent a great deal of time changing her childhood memories and the childhood stories of her parents. Despite trying several different techniques, the feelings of struggle and lack pervaded her revised memories.

Then, during one session, the insight dawned on both of us. Lack and struggle were stories she was holding on to from the country she grew up in. The history of Northern Ireland was full of conflict, suffering, and pain. It seemed obvious. It was the atmosphere she was born into! It was as omnipresent as the air she breathed. What she was holding on to regarding the history of Northern Ireland would have been handed down via parents, school, the church, and her own lived experience.

We started by going back as far as she needed to and changing the story of Northern Ireland. Almost instantly, the dam broke, and she enthusiastically created an island of love, safety, and abundance— changing references of English rule and the famine, all the way to the Struggles from the 1960s to 1990s. Now, in her story, Northern Ireland has always been a country of celebration, parties, and peace. Now all citizens of Northern Ireland are known for their perpetual attitude of fun, love, connection, abundance, and carnival-style parties, which unites the entire country.

As we changed the story and added new, exciting details of the wonderful new story of Northern Ireland, her ability to imagine a new childhood for her parents and herself happened automatically.

What Does it Do?

When we read or are told about something, even if we've never experienced it, the brain forms a memory. Memories are created even though we didn't personally experience the events because the unconscious part of the brain can't tell the difference between reality and imagination.

As we're told about family struggles, war, injustice, poverty, slavery, persecution, and suffering, the brain forms memories. And, depending on what other references are already there, how the stories are told to us, who tells us, and how much emotion is involved, those memories can become part of the "evidence" that "proves" who we are and how the world works. Bearing in mind that the unconscious part of the brain cannot use reason or logic, it cannot therefore filter the information based on reasoning. It filters the information based on the references it already holds.

So, for example, as you hear about the suffering your ancestors experienced, while your conscious mind can comprehend linear time, and you consciously know that those events happened to your ancestors and are not happening to you right now, the unconscious part of your brain cannot do that. Depending on what references are already there, and how you are told about the suffering of your ancestors, that unconscious part of your brain may take that information as "evidence" that "proves" that who you are is a person who suffers. Add to this the natural, automatic drive to fit in with the "tribe" so that you're accepted and not rejected, and you can see how suffering would become an unconscious, automatic survival state – despite your conscious efforts to improve your life.

As you change those implicit memories to the opposite, positive, and empowering (while you're still able to consciously know what originally happened) your brain then strives to keep you in alignment with the new "evidence." Keeping you in alignment with your "tribe" now means keeping you in alignment with that new family history of love, safety, connection, kindness, compassion, abundance, respect, value, joy, freedom, and peace.

How to Rewrite Cultural or Religious History and References

Step One:

You may be unable to imagine your parents and grandparents growing up in an environment of love, kindness, compassion, security, connection, respect, and with an abundance of affection, fun, and support, but regardless, notice what happens when you try.

Step Two:

Whatever comes up about your family background, notice how you know. Were you told? Did you read about it? You may not remember how you know—you may just have images, sounds, or feelings. Just notice what's there.

Step Three:

Imagine those scenes differently. Imagine the opposite, positive, and empowering. Imagine being told how lucky, healthy, happy, and wealthy your ancestors were. Imagine being told how peaceful, joyful, and abundant your country was throughout history. Imagine being told: *"We are so fortunate to have such an empowering heritage. We come from a long line of compassionate and valued people. Our country is known for its abundance and peace. We've always been lucky..."* Whatever would feel empowering and "prove" the life you want to live now.

If you find you're not able to imagine those new memories, again, notice what happens when you try. See what thoughts, feelings, or memories pop up for you and then, of course, change those. Use the Detective Work, and other tools in this book (you may need the Due Justice Technique, for example) to change whatever comes up that is stopping you from imagining these new memories, and then come back to Step Three. Keep repeating this process until you're able to do Step Three.

Step Four:
Repeat those new memories over and over, to establish the new references.

An example from Odille:

A client I worked with a couple of years ago suffered from extreme anxiety. It was almost constant and was keeping her from moving forward toward creating the business she loved. We had changed several negative childhood memories, but she couldn't imagine her parents being happy and relaxed. When I asked her to imagine their childhoods differently, she said she couldn't. I asked her what happened when she tried, and she said that her grandparents on both sides were very strict, and not at all affectionate. She was also unable to imagine their childhoods differently. I asked her what happened when she tried, and she said an image from Sunday School came to her. The teacher was talking about retribution. She couldn't remember the details, but she felt extreme fear, and had visuals of people in a fire.

Without needing to go into any details, I asked her if she could imagine the scene differently—a Stepping-Stone of the teacher telling her about people being rescued from a fire. They were rescued by firefighters and were safe and unharmed. She was able to do this. She repeated that Stepping-Stone a couple of times, and then I asked her if she could imagine that instead of a fire, it was a trampoline. People bouncing on a trampoline. She was able to do that. Again, she repeated it a couple of times. Next, I asked her if she could imagine God hugging the people, that they were surrounded by light and love. She was able to do that and repeated it a couple of times. Finally, I asked her if she could imagine the teacher telling her about God's unconditional love, kindness, and compassion, and the fact that everyone is always safe, and loved, and that there are trampolines for those who want them. This became the final memory that she established, replacing her fear-filled one.

While she still consciously knew what the Sunday School teacher had taught, the unconscious part of her brain no longer held it as "evidence" that "proved" she was always in danger. And it, therefore, no longer triggered a constant level of stress chemicals that caused automatic and constant anxiety. Of course, there were other memories that still supported her anxiety, but as we continued to change those, her levels of anxiety decreased, and she no longer suffered from it.

RECAP:

- Cultural and religious history can be responsible for providing key references that "prove" current issues you're trying to change.
- Changing those memories of religious or cultural pain and struggle is about changing the implicit memories to explicit—in other words, making those memories conscious so that you're able to remember what happened without them defining your life experiences moving forward.

Free to Move Forward

Having freed herself from her debilitating anxiety, Odille's client was now ready to continue toward her goal of becoming a professional photographer. She used Reverse Engineering (Chapter 24), to automatically achieve her goal of turning her passion into a successful business.

Getting Specific:
Reverse Engineering

Although creating new childhood memories of being loved and safe, filled with connection, support, empowerment, respect, fun, freedom, and affection are the foundation of creating any changes you want to make in yourself and your life moving forward, it's possible to home in a little more. Using Reverse Engineering, you can create even more specific references to support results you want to achieve.

When to Use Reverse Engineering

You can either use this technique just because it feels good and adds more substance to your memories, or with a particular goal in mind. Whether you use Reverse Engineering or not will depend on your own preferences.

What Does it Do?

Reverse Engineering your implicit memories will give your brain extra references for specific results you want to achieve and experience now. As you create new memories that "prove" you have a background in whatever it is you want, this exercise gives your brain extra "evidence" for those results.

How to Use Reverse Engineering

Step One:

Think about the results you want to achieve in your life and imagine what it would have been like growing up in a family where you were surrounded by those experiences.

For example: If you want to be fit and healthy now, imagine the experience of growing up in a family where your parents, grandparents, and everyone else was fit and healthy. Can you imagine what meals would have been like? Can you imagine the activities you would have done? Imagine going out, biking, hiking, or doing yoga with your parents from a young age. Whatever it is you'd like your life to be like, now.

If you want to be a successful photographer, imagine having grown up in a family of professional photographers. What would it have been like to be with your parents in the studio or on location? What would it have been like with them teaching you about lighting, composition, and developing? Imagine how it would have felt when they surprised you with your own dream camera. Imagine seeing your parents being awarded for their photographic work.

If you want to be successful in trading or real estate, imagine growing up in a family that loved that profession. Imagine sitting at the table with your parents, in front of their laptop, as they traded. Imagine your parents teaching you how to find good property deals. What would it have been like to go with them to view properties? To learn everything you needed to know to be successful from them? When they surprised you on your seventh birthday with a rental property of your very own? When you were 10 years old and they surprised you with your own bankroll to start using what you'd learned from them to start trading yourself, with their guidance, encouragement, enthusiasm, and support?

NOTE: It doesn't matter if the technology didn't exist when you were growing up—remember, that unconscious part of your brain doesn't know that! It will believe whatever you give it!

Step Two:

Now, create those memories, just by imagining them, and then pick one or two that represent the feeling of growing up with that background. Repeat those couple of new memories over and over until they're established.

Step Three:

Play those new memories (they needn't be long, maybe just a few seconds)—with the feelings—last thing at night, first thing in the morning, and as often as you can during the day, especially whenever you think of those goals you want to achieve. In other words, whenever you think of your dream of being a successful photographer, recall the memory of being with your parents at their gallery when one of your parents gave you your first dream camera. Or the memory of learning about lighting and one of your parents praising you for your photography when you were 10 years old. Whatever creates those feelings inside you of having everything it takes to get what you want because you come from a background that "proves" it.

A few more ideas for Reverse Engineering Memories:

At seven years old, you were the youngest published author in your town, and your parents (successful authors themselves) are bursting with pride during the press event where the three of you are being interviewed about your success.

You remember your parents teaching you in a fun way everything they knew about how to run a business. You remember that running a business was always enjoyable and easy for them. Then, at eight years old, they helped you start your own little business, and you have amazing memories of customers lined up around the block.

You have wonderful memories of how organized your parents were. The house was always beautifully tidy, clean, and organized. You remember friends coming to visit, and saying to you *"Ah, you're so lucky—I wish my house was like this!"* Your parents taught you, from a very young age, how to organize easily and automatically. They gave you tips on making it quick and fun. You can remember the feeling of all three of you laughing together while you created organization systems around the house.

Every morning, when you woke up, your parents would take you with them on their morning run. They were always in a wonderful mood—they loved running and they especially loved being with you. The three of you would run through the most gorgeous places, and you'd love seeing the animals and smelling the scent of grass and flowers in the air. When you got home, you looked forward to the delicious, healthy smoothies and cool, refreshing water. You can remember running your first marathon with your parents, when you were nine years old, and how amazed they were and so proud of you at how well you were able to keep up.

Note: Remember, there's no limit to the budget or special effects inside your mind. So, allow yourself to make these new memories as wonderful as possible. No limits. The more amazing you make them, the more powerful the "evidence" that "proves" the results you want to experience in your life now will be.

You come from a long line of people who_____.

RECAP:

- Reverse Engineering is about intentionally creating specific "evidence" that "proves" what you want to experience in your life, moving forward.
- The unconscious part of your brain will refer to the new evidence, and automatically respond accordingly, leading you toward the results you want in your life now.

Next Steps

Well done for empowering yourself with this knowledge! We're so proud of you for giving yourself the gift of taking control of your own brain. We're so excited for you, for the transformation you'll achieve by giving that little you the childhood you deserved—and should have had.

If you've followed along with the exercises and techniques as you've been reading, you'll have already noticed some of the effects along the way. Now it's important to continue to use them. You are the only boss of your brain. You are the only boss of you.

You may not always have a choice in what happens to you, or around you, but you *do* always have a choice in where you're putting your focus in the moment. It's not always easy, but it *is* always possible. Remember that, just like physical exercise, there will be ups and downs along the way to achieving the results you want.

There are no straight roads from where you are to where you want to be. They're winding, and there are hills and valleys. The information in this book will help you to stay on the road no matter how winding and hilly it may get, and regardless of the storms and diversions you may encounter on that route. It will help you to *enjoy* the journey and experiences along the way, until you reach the transformation you want and deserve.

Keep this book handy. Keep referring to it. Re-read certain sections to really absorb the information. Refer to it whenever things get difficult, or you feel doubt or resistance. And reach out to us for help and support as you go. Join our community on Facebook and contact us through our website or social media. Watch our YouTube videos. You may have reached the end of this book, but we're still here with you. We're still here *for* you.

And we're cheering you on!

With love,
Odille and Steve

Frequently Asked Questions

What do I do when my mind tells me: But that's not what really happened?
The fact that that's not what really happened only matters to the conscious mind. The unconscious part of your brain will believe whatever you give it.

The unconscious part of your brain can't tell the difference between reality and imagination, can't use logic or reason, and can't judge something as unrealistic. When you watch a scary movie, your brain and body behave as if the threat is real: your heart rate increases; adrenaline is pumped into your bloodstream; and you go into the fight-freeze-flight state. And this happens no matter how unrealistic or illogical it may be (dinosaurs, anyone?). At the same time, your conscious mind knows it's just a movie. We don't usually sit through a movie or TV show saying, *"But this isn't real!"* unless it's particularly scary. In the same way, you can allow the unconscious part of your brain to believe the new, empowering childhood memories, while you consciously still know what originally happened.

So, if the thought, *But that's not what really happened* comes up, be sure to answer it with: *Yes, that's true, but the unconscious part of my brain doesn't know that. Just like a movie. And I'm choosing where I want to go, by changing the GPS.*

Is it wrong to change memories?
Is it wrong to change the coordinates in your GPS from where you are now, to where you want to go next?

There are no memory police, and memories are already changing. If you recall a memory right now, from when you were five years old, you are not bringing to mind a complete "movie" or picture. Your brain is, in fact, pulling together a range of resources, and "piecing" that memory together as you recall it. Memories are not stored as complete representations of events. They are put together in the moment you remember them, like a jigsaw puzzle. And the resulting memory is changed as you recall it, according to any new resources gathered since the last time you recalled it.

Just as every new experience is filtered through existing references from previous experiences, memories are filtered through current data from all previous experiences to date.

There are no pictures or movies in the brain. There are no sounds or people in the brain. It's all just cells connecting, and chemical responses to those connections. And, although those connections have been happening automatically without your conscious awareness so far, now you get to choose. You get to choose which neurons you fire and in what patterns— and therefore which chemicals to trigger: stress chemicals or "feel-good" chemicals. And while you're changing the implicit (unconscious) memories, you will retain the explicit (conscious) ones.

What if I don't/can't really recall much of my childhood?

Just start with whatever you *can* remember. Your brain will either automatically change the rest, or you'll find you do start to recall some memories. For example: If the earliest memory you have of feeling frightened is a year ago, that's okay. Address and change that memory, and as you do that, you may find yourself remembering something from your childhood. Then you can change that, too. Always change the earliest memory you can remember first, from whenever that may be. And whatever you do recall, or even just know from being told about it from your childhood, change that. You can also just start with the Bookmark Memories. Create those Bookmark Memories and change any memories or "knowings" that pop up that contradict them.

What if I can't feel any emotions?

If you're changing a negative memory, and you can't feel any negative emotions, that's a good thing. Just imagine the event differently. If you can't feel the positive emotions in the little Beginner's Exercise from Part One of this book, spend more time focusing on that favorite color, and ask yourself what it is you love about the "subject" you chose for that exercise. If that doesn't help, you may want to try a different subject. Remember that all of this is like physical exercise. If you hadn't done much physical exercise before, and you started running or lifting weights, you may find you can't do much. That wouldn't mean you can't do it at all—it would just mean you need more practice to condition your body, to build the stamina and muscles. This is the same. Just because you can't feel the emotions now, doesn't mean you won't ever feel them. It just means you need more practice. If you can't feel the positive emotions in the new memories, zoom in on the details a bit more. The more you focus on details, the more you'll be increasing the level of those "feel-good" chemicals. This is why we don't want to get into the details of a negative memory. But we *do* want to get into the details of the positive ones.

If you still can't feel the positive emotions, try using The Due Justice Technique and / or The Allowing Technique in addition to continuing to practice the Beginner's Exercise.

I'm not visual.

That's okay, just use your "knowing." In other words, if you don't see a memory visually, or can't imagine one, just think about it happening in whatever way you would "know" it happened.

Does the "subject" I use for the brain chemistry exercise have to be the same, or can I change it?

You can change the subject whenever you like. As long as you're able to feel that love and connection, you can use a different subject every time if you wish.

Why am I having trouble accessing the good feelings?

It's probably because the levels of stress chemicals in your system are already high (and stress chemicals are stronger than "feel-good" chemicals, for survival). So, you can't feel the effects of the "feel-good" chemicals yet. As you continue to do the Beginner's Exercise in Part One, and practice Zero Tolerance, you will start to be able to access those good feelings. As the level of stress chemicals lowers over time, you'll also begin to feel the effects of the "feel-good" chemicals.

Another possibility is that the unconscious part of your brain is protecting you by keeping you in high alert to any "danger." Remember that we're wired for survival, so it's more important to focus on the danger than on the good stuff—it's more important to notice the bear than the pretty flowers. Think of that unconscious part of your brain as a dog. This dog has been conditioned to attack anyone that comes near him because of the experiences he's had so far. It will take time, patience, and consistency to train that dog to no longer be constantly in "fight" mode. It will take time and reassurance to recondition the dog to trust people. You are the new owner of the dog, and you now know how to rehabilitate, retrain, and recondition him. Just because the dog is still aggressive when someone comes to the door doesn't mean he'll never be able to react in a friendly, loving way. It just means he needs more training, more time, consistency, and patience.

Recent memories feel stronger than childhood memories. Why should I start with childhood memories?

Your more recent experiences are filtered through your childhood memories. In every moment, the unconscious part of your brain is referring to your implicit childhood memories, to determine what a current experience means, and how to respond. It then triggers chemicals that will affect how you experience the event. If you just change the recent memories (even if the emotions are stronger), the original references from your childhood will still be there, which means you will continue to experience that issue or challenge again. Think of childhood memories as the roots of a weed, and recent memories and experiences as the branches, leaves, and stem of that weed. If you just cut off the branches and leaves—or even the whole stem—the weed will always grow back. You have to remove the roots. If you remove the roots, the rest of the weed is removed automatically.

I feel like I am being disloyal to my family by changing memories.

This is a natural feeling. Ask yourself this: If you had the power to go back in time, with a magic wand, and give all the children in all generations of your family the most wonderful childhood, where they feel safe, loved, and valued, and have an abundance of affection, kindness, compassion, and everything they need—would you do it? Would you give them that gift? You are effectively doing just that because the unconscious part of your brain can't tell the difference between reality and imagination. In addition, no one needs to know you're doing this. This is something you're doing inside your own mind. And any feelings of disloyalty are also happening only inside your own mind. It's no more disloyal than changing the GPS coordinates to your desired destination. You're not denying or disrespecting—or even forgetting—what originally happened. You're setting the desired destination for where you go next. And as you change those memories, you are creating *more* love and compassion in connection with your family.

How long should I practice new memories?

The first time you create a new memory, play it three times in a row. And then practice it regularly until it feels established. This will vary from person to person and from one memory to another. You'll know it's established when, as you think of that event, the new memory with strong positive emotions is the first thing that pops into your mind. Of course, you can never practice too much! Every time you play the new memory with the associated positive emotions, you increase the level of "feel-good" chemicals in your system, and you make that reference—that "evidence"—stronger.

What should I do if the new memories don't feel real?

Zoom in on the details of the new memory. The more you focus on details, the higher the level of matching chemicals will be. This is why we don't focus on the details of the negative memories. We can use the details of the new empowering memories to amp up the feelings. Focus in on the loving expressions and what it is you love about this scenario. Create dialogue, for example, your parents saying: *"I love you so much. We are so grateful to have you as our child!"* If the new memory still doesn't feel real, it may be because there are other references the unconscious part of your brain is holding on to so try using the Anchor Memory Technique or doing the Due Justice Technique. Then, come back to the new memory again, and see if it feels more real.

Am I just living a delusional life doing this work?

Great question! Imagine you are in Chicago, and you want to end up in Los Angeles. When you plan that journey and set your GPS to Los Angeles—even while you're still in Chicago—are you being delusional? As you drive from Chicago toward Los Angeles—even though you're not in Los Angeles yet—are you being delusional? It's true you're not there, right now, but if you don't allow your mind to go to Los Angeles ahead of your body, and you don't put Los Angeles into your GPS (even though that's not where you are now), you'll never get there. Are you delusional when you watch a movie and you allow yourself to get lost in it, feeling the feelings as if the movie is reality? The difference between being delusional and doing this work is that you are not the GPS. You are programming the GPS (the unconscious part of your brain) while you, as the driver, still know where you were before, where you are now, and you are choosing where you go next. This is empowerment.

What does it mean if the old memory keeps coming back?

If you've changed a memory, and the old memory keeps coming back it may mean that your brain has some other "evidence" that is preventing it from changing completely. The solution is to use the Due Justice Technique, and the Anchor Memory Technique.

Does the Remmert Method work on PTSD?

Although the Remmert Method can work on post-traumatic stress disorder (PTSD), we don't recommend addressing trauma on your own. It's important to get help and support from a certified Remmert Method practitioner. The practitioner will take you through the process of finding and changing the original childhood memories that are at the core of the trauma.

A Note on PTSD from experiences as an adult:

It is always childhood experiences that are at the root of PTSD. As we experience trauma in adulthood, the unconscious part of the brain is (as always) referring to childhood implicit memories to determine what the experience means and how to respond. Several people can experience the same traumatic event, but not all of them will suffer from PTSD. What makes the difference is each person's implicit memories from childhood that are informing their self-image and worldview.

Notes

Notes

1. Jonathan L. C. Lee, Karim Nader, & Daniela Schiller. "An Update on Memory Reconsolidation Updating." *Trends in Cognitive Sciences.* 21(7), 2017: 531–45. doi:10.1016/j.tics.2017.04.006.

2. University of Colorado at Boulder. "Your Brain on Imagination: It's a lot like Reality, Study Shows." ScienceDaily. December 10, 2018. www.sciencedaily.com/releases/2018/12/181210144943.htm.

3. Dean Mobbs, Cindy C. Hagan, Tim Dalgleish, Brian Silston, & Charlotte Prévost. "The Ecology of Human Fear: Survival Optimization and the Nervous System." *Frontiers in Neuroscience.* 18(9), 2015: 55. doi:10.3389/fnins.2015.00055.

4. Bruno S. Frey, David A. Savage, & Benno Torgler. "Interaction of Natural Survival Instincts and Internalized Social Norms Exploring the Titanic and Lusitania Disasters." *PNAS.* 107(11), 2010: 4862–65. https://doi.org/10.1073/pnas.0911303107.

5. Abigail A. Marsh. "Neural, Cognitive, and Evolutionary Foundations of Human Altruism." *WIREs Wiley Interdisciplinary Reviews: Cognitive Science.* 7(1), 2016: 59–71. doi:10.1002/wcs.1377.

6. University of California, Los Angeles. "Your Brain Might be Hard-wired for Altruism: Neuroscience Research Suggests an Avenue for Treating the Empathically Challenged." ScienceDaily. March 18, 2016. www.sciencedaily.com/releases/2016/03/160318102101.htm.

7. University of Zurich. "The Evolutionary Roots of Human Altruism." ScienceDaily. August 27, 2014. www.sciencedaily.com/releases/2014/08/140827092002.htm.

8. "The Remmert Method." www.facebook.com/groups/theremmertmethod/

9. John H. Byrne. "Introduction to Neurons and Neuronal Networks." Neuroscience Online. October 10, 2021. https://nba.uth.tmc.edu/neuroscience/m/s1/introduction.html.

10. Amy F. T. Arnsten. "Stress Signalling Pathways that Impair Prefrontal Cortex Structure and Function." *Nature Reviews Neuroscience.* 10(6), 2009: 410–22. doi:10.1038/nrn2648.

11. "Implicit Memory." ScienceDirect. https://www.sciencedirect.com/topics/social-sciences/implicit-memory.

12. Marianne E. Lloyd & Jeremy K. Miller. "Implicit Memory." APA Psychnet. In P. J. Bauer & R. Fivush (Eds). *The Wiley Handbook on the Development of Children's Memory* (pp. 336–59). (Hoboken, NJ: Wiley Blackwell). https://psycnet.apa.org/record/2013-26762-015.

13. Henry Otgaar, Alan Scoboria, & Tom Smeets. "Experimentally Evoking Nonbelieved Memories for Childhood Events," *Journal of Experimental Psychology: Learning, Memory, and Cognition.* 39(3), 2013: 717–30: https://doi.org/10.1037/a0029668.

14. Jose Silva. (1991). *The Silva Mind Control Method.* (New York, NY: Pocket Books).

15. Joseph Murphy. (Reissue edition, 2019). *The Power of Your Subconscious Mind.* (New York, NY: Simon & Schuster).

16. Robert G. Smith "Faster EFT." www.fastereft.com.

17. David R. Hamilton. https://d.facebook.com/319102607782/photos/a.1015 9605830952783/10159605830922783/?type=3&source=57.

18. Tony Robbins. "How To Make a Massive Action Plan (MAP)." Tony Robbins. Accessed on October 11, 2021. https://www.tonyrobbins.com/career-business/how-to-make-a-massive-action-plan-map/.

19. Louise Hay. "What Is Mirror Work?" Louise Hay. Accessed on October 11, 2021. https://www.louisehay.com/what-is-mirror-work.

20. Esther Hicks. (2005). *The Law of Attraction: The Basics of the Teachings of Abraham.* (Carlsbad, CA: Hay House Inc.).

21. Rhonda Byrne. (2008). *The Secret.* (London: Simon & Schuster).

22. William Arntz, Betsy Chasse, Mark Vicente, dirs. *What the Bleep Do We Know?* (Phoenix: Roadside Attraction & Samuel Goldwyn Films, 2004), documentary.

23. Lou Whitaker, "How Does Thinking Positive Thoughts Affect Neuroplasticity?" Meteor Education. https://meteoreducation.com/how-does-thinking-positive-thoughts-affect-neuroplasticity/. Accessed October 10, 2021.

24. Brianna Chu, Komal Marwaha, Terrence Sanvictores, & Derek Ayers. "Physiology, Stress Reaction." StatPearls. (2021). https://www.ncbi.nlm.nih.gov/books/NBK541120.

25. Joseph E. LeDoux & Richard Brown. "A Higher-Order Theory of Emotional Consciousness." *PNAS.* 114(10), 2017: E2016–25. https://doi.org/10.1073/pnas.1619316114.

26. David S. Goldstein. "Adrenal Responses to Stress." *Cellular and Molecular Neurobiology.* 30(8), 2010:1433–40. doi:10.1007/s10571-010-9606-9. https://www.ncbi.nlm.nih.gov/pmc/articles/PMC3056281.

27. Samuel T. Moulton & Stephen M. Kosslyn. "Imagining Predictions: Mental Imagery as Mental Emulation." *Philos Trans R Soc Lond B Biol Sci.* 364(1521), 2009:1273–80. doi: 10.1098/rstb.2008.0314.https://pubmed.ncbi.nlm.nih.gov/19528008.

28. Oprah Winfrey & Bruce Perry. (2021). *What Happened to You?* (Flatiron Books: An Oprah Book)

29. Bruce Ecker. "Memory Reconsolidation Understood and Misunderstood." *International Journal of Neuropsychotherapy.* 3(1), 2015: 2–46.doi: 10.12744/ijnpt.2015.0002-0046.

30. Donna J. Bridge & Ken. A Paller. "Neural Correlates of Reactivation and Retrieval-Induced Distortion." *Journal of Neuroscience.* 32(35), 2012:12144–151. https://www.jneurosci.org/content/32/35/12144.

31. Julia Shaw. (2016). *The Memory Illusion: Remembering, Forgetting, and the Science of False Memory.* (Canada: Doubleday).

32. Emiliano Merlo, Amy L. Milton, & Barry J. Everitt. "Enhancing Cognition by Affecting Memory Reconsolidation." *Current Opinion in Behavioral Sciences.* 4, 2015: 41–47. https://doi.org/10.1016/j.cobeha.2015.02.003.

33. RIKEN. "Fishing For Memories: How Long-Term Memories are Processed to Guide Behavior." ScienceDaily. May 2013. www.sciencedaily.com/releases/2013/05/130516123914.htm.

34. "Preventing Adverse Childhood Experiences." Center for Disease Control and Prevention. April 6, 2021. https://www.cdc.gov/violenceprevention/aces/fastfact.html.

35. Eberhard Fuchs & Gabriele Flügge. "Adult Neuroplasticity: More Than 40 Years of Research", *Neural Plasticity*. 2014, Article ID541870, 10 pages. https://doi.org/10.1155/2014/541870.

36. James L. McGaugh. "Making Lasting Memories: Remembering the Significant." *PNAS*. 110 (Supplement 2), 2013: 10402–07. https://www.pnas.org/content/110/Supplement_2/10402.

37. Tom Bilyeu. "Impact Theory." Impact Theory. https://impacttheory.com/. Accessed October 10, 2021.

38. Institute of Science and Technology Austria. "Neuroscientists Discover New Learning Rule for Pattern Completion." ScienceDaily. www.sciencedaily.com/releases/2016/05/160513111839.htm.

39. Christian Keysers & Valeria Gazzola. "Hebbian Learning and Predictive Mirror Neurons for Actions, Sensations, and Emotions." *Philos Trans R Soc Lond B Biol Sci*. 369(1644), 2014: doi: 10.1098/rstb.2013.0175.

40. Paré, Denis. "Role of the Basolateral Amygdala in Memory Consolidation." *Progress in Neurobiology*. 70(5), 2003: 409–20. https://doi.org/10.1016/S0301-0082(03)00104-7.

41. "Editing Memories." Futureproof with John McCrea, August 1, 2020. Podcast. https://www.newstalk.com/podcasts/futureproof-with-jonathan-mccrea/editing-memories.

42. Margaret Jaworski. "The Negativity Bias: Why the Bad Stuff Sticks." Psycom. https://www.psycom.net/negativity-bias. Accessed October 10, 2021.

43. Anil Kumar, Puneet Rinwa, Gurleen Kaur, & Lalit Machawal. "Stress: Neurobiology, Consequences and Management." *J Pharm Bioallied Sci*. 5(2), 2013:91–97. https://www.ncbi.nlm.nih.gov/pmc/articles/PMC3697199/.

44. Rick Hanson. "Take in the Good." The Practical Science of Lasting Happiness. www.rickhanson.net/take-in-the-good/.

45. James Clear. (2016). *Atomic Habits: An Easy & Proven Way to Build Good Habits & Break Bad Ones.* (New York, NY: Avery).

46. Joseph LeDoux. (2003). *Synaptic Self: How Our Brains Become Who We Are.* (New York, NY: Penguin Books).

47. John M. Allman. (1999). *Evolving Brains.* (New York, NY: Scientific American Library).

48. Andrea Ballesio & Nicola Cellini. "Updating Internal Cognitive Models During Sleep." *Journal of Neuroscience.* 39(11), 2019:1966–68. doi: https://doi.org/10.1523/JNEUROSCI.2926-18.2019.

49. University of Texas at Austin. "New study decodes brain's process for decision making." ScienceDaily. November 2013. www.sciencedaily.com/releases/2013/11/131108112144.htm.

Acknowledgements

From Odille:

A special thank you to my sister, Sharelle, without whom I literally wouldn't still be alive. In addition to being there for me, in too many ways to count, a lot of the techniques, tools, and insights we share in this book have come from her wisdom.

From Odille and Steve:

A big thank you to Robert G. Smith, founder of eutaptics® and FasterEFT™, from whom we first learned about the effects of childhood memories on the adult, and (most importantly) that those memories can be changed. Although we share the scientific references we've found since then at the end of this book, it was Robert who first taught us, not only that it's possible to change memories, but how to change them.

To our clients and community members, without whom much of what we share in this book wouldn't exist. Every step we've made in developing these techniques and tools into what they are now, has been because of you. Every question you've asked, every request for clarification, every time you reached out to us for more help and additional solutions has resulted in the information in this book that will help countless others. Thank you!

Further Resources

Visit our website for more information and resources:
www.TheRemmertMethod.com

Download the Generational Childhood Memory Transformation Meditation Guide:
https://www.theremmertmethod.com/extra-resources

Watch our videos on YouTube:
https://www.youtube.com/c/TheRemmertMethod

Reach out to us for help, through our Facebook Group:
https://www.facebook.com/groups/theremmertmethod

Watch the recordings of live group sessions, and download the audio guide of the little brain-chemistry exercise, here:
https://www.theremmertmethod.com/emotional-fitness-resources.html

Criminal Psychologist and Memory Scientist, Julia Shaw specializes in false memory. She shares her experience with deliberately creating false memories, and how that works, in this TEDx Talk: "Is Your Memory Just an Illusion?"
https://youtu.be/owAeCKiM_4A

Director of the Memories in Neuropsychiatric Disorders Lab in the Department of Psychology at the University of Cambridge, Amy Milton shares her research on changing memories (Memory Reconsolidation) to

treat PTSD in this TED Talk: "Destroying Memories: How this could Improve our Mental Health."
https://youtu.be/a8vxE6EqRM4

Jill Bolte Taylor. (2021). *Whole Brain Living.* (Carlsbad, CA: Hay House Inc).